ABSOLUTE KNOWLEDGE

for Michael Walzer.

28 Jan. 1985

ABSOLUTE KNOWLEDGE:

Hegel and the Problem of Metaphysics

ALAN WHITE

OHIO UNIVERSITY PRESS
ATHENS, OHIO
LONDON

Library of Congress Cataloging in Publication Data

White, Alan, 1951–
　　Absolute knowledge.

　　Bibliography: p.
　　1. Hegel, Georg Wilhelm Friedrich, 1770–1831.
2. Schelling, Friedrich Wilhelm Joseph von,
1775–1854.　I. Title.
B2948.W47　1983　　　　　　193　　　　　82–22449
ISBN 0–8214–0717–1
ISBN 0–8214–0718–X (pbk.)

For Jane

Table of Contents

Preface

In writing this book, I have attempted to be intelligible to the reader lacking specific philosophical background without thereby boring the philosopher or the scholar. I do not believe that accounts accessible to laymen need be superficial, particularly when the accounts deal with thinkers as difficult as Hegel, whose doctrines have been understood in so many different ways that any interpretation must be carefully explained and grounded if it is to be of real interest even to initiates. At the same time, discussion on a level of interest to the specialist need not be presented in such a way that it cannot serve the student as well; indeed, "introductions" that assertorically relate "what Hegel meant" or "the essence of German Idealism" without probing difficult theoretical and systematic issues do not truly serve to introduce. Readers unacquainted with Hegel's works may feel themselves briefly at a loss as they begin to read Chapter One—the criticism of Hegel seeming to presuppose knowledge of what is criticized—but the feeling should have vanished by the end of the chapter's second subsection, "Speculative Logic as the First Science."

Acknowledgments

Since teachers cannot be thanked adequately, they should be thanked frequently. Edward Ballard taught me, when I was an undergraduate, that philosophy neither begins nor ends with Wittgenstein. Stanley Rosen taught me, several years later, to view the history of philosophy as a series, not of quite different sets of problems, but of alternative solutions to the same problems. Thomas Seebohm taught me how the transcendental philosopher approaches those problems, and revealed to me the promise of that approach. Klaus Hartmann taught me, first through his works and then through classes and discussions, to understand Hegel as a transcendental philosopher.

It is a great privilege for me to be able to express publicly my gratitude to my teachers, particularly Rosen and Seebohm, with whom I studied longest and hardest. For financial support during part of the time in which this book was in preparation, I thank the Pennsylvania State University and the German Academic Exchange Service (D.A.A.D.).

Those who consider the Devil to be a partisan of Evil and angels to be warriors for Good accept the demagogy of the angels. Things are clearly more complicated.

Angels are partisans not of Good, but of divine creation. The Devil, on the other hand, denies all rational meaning to God's world.

World domination, as everyone knows, is divided between demons and angels. But the good of the world does not require the latter to gain precedence over the former (as I thought when I was young); all it needs is a certain equilibrium of power. If there is too much uncontested meaning on earth (the reign of the angels), man collapses under the burden; if the world loses all its meaning (the reign of the demons), life is every bit as impossible.

—Milan Kundera

Introduction: First Philosophy

PHYSICS AND METAPHYSICS

Over a century and a half ago, Georg Wilhelm Friedrich Hegel audaciously claimed that he had completed philosophy, satisfying the love of wisdom by attaining absolute knowledge. The claim is easily refuted by sophomoric students who point to the existence of Nietzsche and Wittgenstein to prove that philosophy did not end with Hegel, but attempted refutations that do not bother to determine what might really be meant by those against whom they are directed are not to be taken seriously. Moreover, no matter how Hegel may have understood his claim, in a certain historical sense philosophy does terminate with his system: whereas he presents that system as the culmination of a coherent tradition that began in ancient Greece, the most notorious post-Hegelian thinkers—including Marx, Kierkegaard, Nietzsche, and Heidegger—explicitly oppose that tradition. In addition, Hegel was the last thinker able to convince his contemporaries that the highest theoretical endeavor, that which grounds all others, is *prote philosophia*—first philosophy—rather than mathematics or physics. Whether or not Hegel's absolute knowledge successfully completes the philosophical tradition, then, it does in a sense bring it to its end.

After Hegel's time, first philosophy, traditionally known as metaphysics, is no longer revered as queen of the sciences. Its deposition is often taken as a sign of intellectual progress; positivists from Comte onwards have insisted that metaphysics is a naive and confused mode of theorizing that has been completely replaced by the mathematical–empirical sciences, and regardless of

1

the degree of cogency of the positivists' arguments, their conclusion is supported by the manifest superiority of the sciences to most of what passes at present for philosophy. Scientific investigation is of far more immediate importance than is the scholarly analysis—either of language and meaning or of obscure texts—that tends to occupy the contemporary academic philosopher, and the sciences exhibit a rational coherence that is entirely absent from the eulogies of mystic fulfillments that crowd the philosophy shelves in shopping-mall bookstores.

Be the causes and the legitimacy of the development as they may, it remains a matter of historical fact that metaphysics is no longer respected as the highest theoretical endeavor. Yet even if the object of that respect is now mathematical physics, that science cannot occupy the position from which metaphysics has ostensibly been ousted, and for at least two reasons. First, while metaphysics purports or attempts to ground *all* knowledge, including that of its own principles, both physics and mathematics rely on methodological principles that can be neither deductively proved nor empirically established. If these principles are not to be dogmatically presupposed, they must be supported by argumentation that is neither merely formal nor merely empirical; they must be supported by arguments that can be developed and evaluated in no domain save that of philosophy.[1] Second, and much more obvious, is the inability of any mathematical or empirical science to appropriate the metaphysical task of grounding ethics: precisely that aspect of the sciences that has made them so tremendously successful—the insistence on objectivity, the concentration on facts alone—excludes from their realm of consideration all questions of absolute value. The sciences give us information that can be applied to various ends; they cannot tell us which ends we should attempt to attain.

For these reasons, the abandonment of metaphysics involves more than the redefinition of the nature of rational inquiry in accordance with the tenets of modern scientific methodology; this redefinition itself makes matters of value and validity mere matters of opinion. Metaphysics cannot be truly replaced by any science that ignores the fundamental metaphysical questions. If it is abandoned, all that is left is what Plato called *philodoxa*—the love of opinion—the attempt to ease the intellectual unrest caused by questions of absolute validity, value, and significance by means of answers that, while not rationally grounded, may nonetheless, at least for a while, be believed. If, after Hegel, first philosophy is no longer queen of the sciences, if even philosophers have come to see their discipline as the sciences' handmaiden, if, as Heidegger has suggested, philosophy is at present involved in the vain attempt to survive its own suicide[2]—then the throne that metaphysics once claimed to occupy is left vacant.

If it is admitted that to accept the abandonment of metaphysics is to admit that our knowledge of facts and values cannot be rationally grounded—and thereby that this knowledge is ultimately indistinguishable from mere opinion—then it should also be granted that metaphysics would be a desirable science even if it were an impossible one. It is the central contention of this study that metaphysics is not impossible if it is understood as Hegelian transcendental ontology. The function of the rest of this introductory chapter is to clarify the meaning of that contention, and to indicate how it is to be supported.

ONTOLOGY AND THEOLOGY

To anyone unfamiliar with the Western philosophical tradition, the assertion that metaphysics is possible as Hegelian transcendental ontology will be simply meaningless; to those who have studied that tradition, it may well appear to be contradictory. It is, after all, Immanuel Kant who is responsible for transcendental philosophy, and Hegel is known as one of Kant's most violent critics. In addition, whereas "metaphysics" has been used over the years in so many different ways that it has little immediate explanatory value, "ontology" is hardly less ambiguous, and so might seem to simply add obscurity to obscurity. All readers, then, regardless of their philosophical sophistication, will be served by a brief historical consideration explaining how I use these terms in this study.

Near the beginning of the Western philosophical tradition, Aristotle argued that first philosophy—the highest theoretical endeavor, the science that aims at wisdom—must be the science of first principles and causes. In the course of his first-philosophical reflections, christened "metaphysics" only years after his death, Aristotle develops two sciences that can lay claim to being fundamental: one, the study (*logos*) of being (*on*) qua being—rather than of any specific sort of being—came, quite understandably, to be termed *ontology*; the other, the study of the highest being (*theos*)—the cause or ground of existence of all beings—is termed by Aristotle himself *theology*. Aristotle's arguments suggest that metaphysics must include both ontology and theology, but they do not reveal how the two sciences are related. Heidegger has insisted that the unresolved tension between them is determinative throughout the history of philosophy. Metaphysics is, he argues, onto-theology.

By the early eighteenth century, the two metaphysical disciplines had in a sense become four: Christian Wolff terms ontology, as the study of categories relevant to beings of all sorts, *general* metaphysics; in Wolff's system, theology joins rational psychology and cosmology in constituting *special* metaphysics, the study of the supersensible beings God, the soul, and the world as an absolute whole. For much of his life, Kant was a Wolffian metaphysician, but he came to realize that Wolff's doctrines are completely vulnerable to objections grounded in empiricists' claims that all human knowledge derives from sensory experience. In the empiricist view, there can be no metaphysics, either general or special. Because categories are arbitrarily abstracted from experience, they can be, at best, useful with respect to that experience, but there can be no ontological science of them, nor can their applicability to supersensible entities—such as Wolff's God, soul, and world—be established. Nor, the argument continues, can human beings have any knowledge of anything they cannot perceive with their senses, and there can therefore be no science at all of the supersensible.

Confronted with these objections, Kant attempts to save metaphysics as first philosophy by transforming it into ontology, by placing knowledge of the supersensible beyond the limits of the theoretical reason of human beings. Kant thus acknowledges the empiricists' contention that knowledge is dependent upon perception, but he denies that perception can be understood as a process in which the subject is simply passive and receptive. Regardless of the nature of the impetus provided the subject from the side of what is perceived, the subject itself contributes to the perception both the forms of sensibility that make the object accessible, and the conceptual forms that make possible the integration of awareness of the object into the unity of the subject's consciousness. These forms are not posterior to experience, nor are they arbitrarily abstracted from it; they are rather among the conditions for the possibility of experience. These conditions are not immediately apparent, but they are accessible to the philosopher who reflects on the phenomenon of experience as a whole; the study of these conditions is termed by Kant *transcendental*. This first-philosophical study is completely distinct from *transcendent* metaphysics, the study of supersensible entities.

Kant's transcendental philosophy attempts to ground knowledge in the realms of mathematics and the empirical sciences, as well as in ordinary sensory experience, and thereby to satisfy one of the requirements of first philosophy that cannot be satisfied by any merely formal or empirical discipline. Kant however does not satisfy the metaphysical requirement of grounding *all* knowledge, for he reflects only on the conditions of possibility of *experience*, and not on the conditions of possibility of *transcendental philosophy*; he attempts to ground knowledge acquired through sensory experience, but not knowledge acquired through reflection on that experience. Furthermore, Kant's first philosophy makes no claim of grounding value judgments. For Kant, values are not known by theoretical reason; they are rather demanded by practical reason.

It was the goal of the post-Kantian German Idealists to develop a first philosophy that would ground itself, and that would also interrelate the theoretical and the practical; it is by producing such a doctrine that Hegel claims to have completed philosophy. To say that the doctrine is *ontological* is to say that it is a doctrine of categories rather than one of supersensible entities (in Wolffian terms, it is general rather than special metaphysics); to say that it is *transcendental* is to say that it presents conditions of possibility of experience, and that the conditions are discovered through philosophical reflection; to say, finally, that this transcendental ontology is *Hegelian* is to emphasize that it overcomes the limitations of Kantianism, that it grounds knowledge in the realms of the transcendental and the practical as well as in that of the empirical.[3]

The meaning of the claim that Hegelian metaphysics is transcendental ontology should now be at least generally clear. To make the claim intelligible is not, however, to make it plausible, much less to establish its truth. Many scholars would insist—many have insisted—that Hegel's metaphysics, culminating as it does with Absolute Spirit, is unquestionably theological, and would reject any assertions to the contrary as simply absurd. One way of countering this objection would be to argue that, despite the evidence to the contrary provided by the multiplicity of interpretations that have been championed over the past hundred and fifty years, the Hegelian texts are unambiguous; the argument would be that careful analysis reveals that only the ontological interpretation is justifiable. This approach is unappealing for, as the variety of interpretations suggests, many of Hegel's phrasings *are* ambiguous. Arguments to the contrary are unlikely to be compelling. I therefore do not attempt to show that Hegel's texts *must* be read ontologically; I rather attempt to establish that if *and only if* the fundament of his system is so interpreted can it stand as a consequent first philosophy. I make the attempt by defending Hegel's teaching from the attack developed by the most important of his contemporaries, Friedrich Wilhelm Joseph Schelling.

HEGEL AND SCHELLING

There are several reasons for my choice of Schelling's critique as a means of approach to Hegel. One is that Schelling occupies the central position within the historical and philosophical nexus connecting Hegel's claimed completion of philosophy with the post-Hegelian abandonment of metephysics. That position is indicated by the facts, discussed in detail in recent studies, that he is the first Hegel critic of note; that within his critique may be found, in at least rudimentary form, all of the fundamental criticisms of Hegel that have ever been made; and that within his positive teachings are visible practical and existential concerns that make intelligible the transition to Feuerbach, Kierkegaard, and Engels, all of whom attended lectures given by Schelling in the years following Hegel's death, and all of whom were receptive to his critique of Hegel, if not to his own estimation of the implications of that critique.[4] A brief consideration of Schelling's basic objections will indicate that there are methodological as well as philosophical and historical reasons for using his critique as a means of approach to Hegel.

Schelling's critique of Hegel develops in two stages. It contains first what I will call a critique of Hegel's *system*, that is, an attack that attempts to establish that the principles of the system entail its internal collapse; and second, a critique of Hegel's *project*, an argument that the entire undertaking is misguided in that, even if it could be and were completed, it would not satisfy the demands of philosophy. The first part of the critique, the critique of the system, focuses on the system's fundament, the *Science of Logic*: the critique is designed to establish that the *Logic* cannot ground both itself and a comprehensive system. Schelling argues that the starting point of the *Logic* is arbitrary and rests on unrecognized presuppositions, that the method of the work is externally applied to contents dogmatically appropriated from Wolff, and that the move from the *Logic* to the Philosophies of Nature and Spirit, which complete the system, is wholly unwarranted. In arguing these points, Schelling is fully cognizant of the seeming ambiguity of Hegel's undertaking. Schelling acknowledges that the *Logic* at times appears to be an ontological work, at times a theological one; he recognizes that some passages suggest that it is a doctrine of categories, others that it is an attempt to explain either the emanation of the finite from the infinite, or the creation of the factical by the absolute. Schelling's critique, unlike those offered by many later thinkers, is not vitiated by any presupposition concerning the nature of the *Logic*. In his critique, Schelling argues that the *Logic* is defective no matter how it is interpreted.

The successful defense of Hegel's system from Schelling's critique must determine the sense in which the *Logic* can function as first philosophy. The analysis below confirms Schelling's contention that the *Logic* utterly fails as transcendent theology, but it also reveals that, interpreted as transcendental ontology, the work is fully defensible from the Schellingian objections. So interpreted, the *Logic* is in principle cogent in the three respects identified by Schelling as crucial: Chapter One of this study reveals that the onset is truly and non-arbitrarily presuppositionless; Chapter Two, that the dialectic—the mode of development—is internal to a content whose source is non-objectionable; and Chapter Three, that the conclusion of the work at once confirms the *Logic*'s own relative completeness and grounds the development to the systematic subsciences of Nature and Spirit. The argument reveals that the subsciences, as grounded in the *Logic*, must also be interpreted ontologically; if consequent, Hegel's system remains on the level of *general* metaphysics throughout.

With the successful defense of the *Logic* from Schelling's critique, Part One of this study is complete. That defense establishes that the work can function as first philosophy if and only if it is taken as an attempt to exhaustively account for the fundamental determinations of thought—the ontological categories—and to establish that these determinations of thought are also the determinations of things. In defending the *Logic*, I do not argue that the work, as it stands, is free from defects; even Hegel never insisted that the *Logic is* flawless, only that it could, in principle, *be made* flawless. Following Hegel, I argue that the *Logic*, if interpreted ontologically, does not contain the crippling flaws identified by Schelling, and thereby that it is a viable first philosophy.

Coming in an age in which the predominant conviction is that there is *no* viable form for first philosophy, the conclusion of Part One—the conclusion that Hegelian ontology *is* viable—is of considerable importance in itself. Nevertheless, that conclusion solves at best the problem of *Hegelian* metaphysics, it is not a solution for the problem of metaphysics as such. The defense of Hegel's *system* from Schelling's critique reveals that if and only if the path followed by the *Logic* is ontological rather than theological can the work, in principle, reach its destination. The question remains of whether that destination is the destination that philosophy does, or should, seek. This is the question raised by Schelling in his critique of Hegel's project; that critique is considered below in Part Two.

Whereas the conflict considered in Part One concerns only the nature of Hegelianism, that discussed in Part Two relates to the function of metaphysics and the nature of philosophy itself. The question is no longer that of whether Hegel's system satisfies its own criteria, it becomes that of whether it satisfies philosophy's criteria. The question could be answered easily only if we knew in advance precisely what philosophy's criteria are, and those of us who are not already in possession of the highest truth do not. Since metaphysics, unlike physics or mathematics, purports to ground its own principles, the problems of the metaphysician's goal and of the criteria that must be met if the goal is to be reached are themselves metaphysical—first-philosophical—problems. We beg the question against Hegel if we begin with the assumption that any successful system must solve problems x, y, and z, and then search Hegel's writings for such solutions. This does not mean that we have no criteria for judging Hegel's success save Hegel's own criteria. It means rather that we must question whatever criteria we introduce, that we cannot simply rely on them. In judging the extent of Hegel's success, it is particularly instructive to use Schelling's metaphysical criteria, and his way of attempting to meet those criteria; consideration of Schelling's own teachings clarifies Hegel's position. The critical comparison of Schelling's program with Hegel's casts light on the philosophical endeavor itself, and thereby facilitates discussion of the extent to which Hegel's system completes that endeavor.

Schelling's final project—which culminates with the metaphysics he named "positive philosophy"—is not one among many that could equally well be compared with Hegel's. Rather, positive philosophy is the Western philosophical tradition's last metaphysics, and it is the only metaphysics, in the classical sense, that is chronologically post-Hegelian. Indeed, Hegelian ontology and Schellingian theology are—as is concretely shown below[5]— the fundamental alternatives for metaphysics in the wake of Kant; historically, the conflict between these two systems is the final metaphysical conflict. Through the way in which Schelling presented his alternative to Hegel, he mediated the historical abandonment of both ontology and theology, and thus of metaphysics itself.

In introducing his system and in his critique of Hegel, Schelling emphasized precisely those difficulties that led post-Idealistic thinkers to reject the metaphysical tradition, difficulties centering on the relations of theory to practice, and of man to the absolute. Schelling insisted that any ontologically grounded teaching must be ultimately nihilistic—it will be unable to establish rational distinctions of absolute value[6]—and that any ontological system will therefore be incapable of showing human beings what they should do. He insisted that Hegel, concentrating on his ontological absolute, had ignored the anthropological and practical problems that are of central importance to human beings and, therefore, to philosophy. Schelling argued these points well enough to convince most of those who heard him lecture, but at the same time, his presentation of his own metaphysics revealed that he himself could not treat the problems he had so effectively emphasized. He did not show, finally, either how his transcendent theology could ground a rational practical doctrine, or how his account of God could develop into an account of man. Schelling's explicit critique of ontology, in conjunction with his unintended *reductio ad impossibilium* of theology, prepared the way for Marxism and existentialism by effectively convincing those who followed that since first philosophy can be neither ontology nor theology, it must be some form of anthropology.[7] It is this conviction that led to the rejection of the classical metaphysical tradition.

Schelling's positive philosophy, as well as his critique of Hegel, has received much scholarly attention in recent years. Since the 1955 publication of Walter Schulz's *The Completion of German*

Idealism in Schelling's Late Philosophy, few have doubted either that the Hegel critique is successful, or that Schelling's final system surpasses Hegel's. Scholarly attention has been focused on how the critique influenced later thinkers, and on the manner in which positive philosophy transcends Hegelianism.[8] I reject both of these key assumptions of recent Schelling scholarship. In Part One, I show that Hegel's *Logic*, if ontologically interpreted, does not fall to Schelling's attack; in Part Two, I show that Schellingian theology is not a viable alternative to Hegelian ontology. I argue in addition, however, that although Hegel ignored the demands on philosophy emphasized by Schelling, the contemporary Hegelian need not, and should not, ignore those demands. In order to facilitate comprehension and evaluation of these various arguments, I indicate in advance how they are developed.

Schelling's objection to Hegel's project is, in essence, that the path that *leads to* ontology *ends with* ontology, and that ontology alone cannot satisfy the demands of the philosopher. Chapter Four develops Schelling's claim that if Hegel's system is ontological, then it is essentially limited. It must be, Schelling insists, because it is a science of abstract essence that remains blind to problems of concrete existence: Hegelian ontology is concerned only with categories or forms, and not with the real beings that may or may not fall under different categories or instantiate different forms. For this reason, Hegel's system can encompass neither a true theology, one that would establish the existence of God as the real ground of the world, nor a true anthropology, one that would treat the problems encountered by finite, temporal human beings existing in an often irrational world. Philosophy can become anthropology, Schelling insists, only if it begins with theology rather than with ontology.

Chapter Five presents Schelling's positive philosophy, the theological metaphysics designed to overcome the limitations of Hegelianism. I include a very brief account of Schelling's early development, because some understanding of that development facilitates comprehension of positive philosophy itself.[9] I then develop an analysis of positive philosophy sufficiently detailed to reveal that system as the theological counterpart to Hegelian ontology, that is, as the second post-Kantian alternative for the metaphysician. The analysis reveals that Schelling's alternative is not a viable one.

If the paths to Schellingian theology and Hegelian ontology are the only metaphysical paths left open by Kant's critique, and if Schelling's path cannot reach its goal, then Hegel's path may be the only path even if, as Schelling insists, it leads no farther than to ontology. The questions of whether it need lead farther and whether it could lead farther are raised in Chapter Six, which examines the nature of Hegelian wisdom. The conclusion of Chapter Six, and of this study as a whole, is that while Hegel himself, concerned primarily with what cannot be otherwise rather than with what in fact is, felt no need to move beyond ontology and therefore did not develop a practical doctrine intended to guide human actions, the Hegelian system nevertheless provides the ground for such a doctrine, and there are good reasons for asserting that the practical doctrine should be developed. The conclusion is that while Hegel is right in embracing transcendental ontology and in rejecting transcendent theology—in opting for general rather than special metaphysics—he is wrong in not seeking to move from his completed ontology to a concrete, practical anthropology. In stressing anthropological problems, Schelling shows more clearly than Hegel where philosophy must end, but it is Hegel who shows the way philosophy must take to reach its end. My argument is that there is no necessity, either logical or philosophical, for the Hegelian to remain sheltered in the realm of the categorial absolute, that rather this absolute is precisely what the philosopher needs to ground further inquiry into those practical and anthropological problems that were crucial to the late Schelling—and to those who came after—but were ignored or left undeveloped by Hegel. While defending Hegel's first philosophy, then, I insist that it is only first philosophy, that it is not all of philosophy; while denying that Hegel completed philosophy by solving all philosophical problems, I argue that the reconsideration of Hegel's metaphysical teachings is an essential step toward philosophical progress in an anti-philosophical, purportedly post-metaphysical age.

PART ONE

The Hegelian System

1

The Beginning

PROBLEMS OF PRESUPPOSITIONLESSNESS

Schelling's Critique

The essence of any philosopher's teaching must be sought, according to Schelling, in his grounding thought (*Grundgedanke*), the fundamental principle from which his more specific doctrines follow. Hegel's grounding thought is, he continues, that "reason relates itself to the in-itself or essence of things, from which it immediately follows that philosophy, insofar as it is rational science, concerns only the 'what' of things, their essence."[1] Schelling's contention is supported by Hegel's description of the *Science of Logic*—the first philosophy of his system—as a science of "pure essences," a "system of concepts" or of "determinations of thought."[2] If however philosophy is for Hegel a science of *essences*—one concerning only the *what* of things, and not the *that*—then the question arises of how he can justify excluding problems of *existence* from his system. Schelling denies that Hegel offers any justification at all for the exclusion: the demands that philosophy "withdraw into pure thinking, and that it accept as its sole immediate object the pure concept," are mere demands, they have no scientific status (10:127); the claim that the absolute is to be found in and by pure thought is an arbitrary presupposition rather than an established result.[3]

If Hegel simply presupposes that philosophy is a science of essences, then his system's claims to absoluteness are seriously compromised; to the extent that the system's principle is arbitrarily chosen, the system itself will be arbitrary. Hegel insists that the *Logic* presupposes neither its principle nor anything else; Schelling denies that such presuppositionlessness is possible, particularly for a science of concepts. First, Hegel accepts without question the "maxims of the most comfortable rationalism," according to which the fundamental concepts are innate ideas that are known directly by reason (10:162). Had Hegel considered the problem of the status of these concepts, Schelling argues, he would have realized that their science cannot be *first* in any system: since concepts exist only for consciousness, the development of the latter out of nature should be treated prior to consideration of the concepts as such. Schelling also denies that concepts are innate ideas;[4] they are, rather, abstracted from the real entities encountered in sensory experience, and are, as such, posterior to those entities (10:140).

As abstractions, concepts are posterior not only to the things from which they are abstracted, they are also posterior to—and dependent upon—the subject who constructs them. The subject poses further problems for Hegel's science of essences. No philosopher intends to present a doctrine that is "subjective" in the pejorative sense—a doctrine that is arbitrary—but the German Idealists generally, following Kant, were convinced that philosophy must be grounded in the subject rather than in any object. That the subject must be explicitly posited at the very beginning of any potentially comprehensive dialectical movement—that it can never be derived from the object—is one of the arguments with which Fichte had grounded his subjective idealism nearly twenty years before the appearance of Hegel's *Logic*. Hegel and Schelling were both strongly drawn to Fichte's teachings in their youth, but the young Schelling argued—with Hegel's support—that Fichte, in rejecting the objective as a systematic starting point, went too far toward the other extreme: he attempted to ground his account in the *individual human subject*, and was then unable to derive a true objectivity. The young Schelling attempted to rectify the error by beginning with the self-objectification of the *absolute*—rather than the merely human—subject: in his account, subjective and objective moments are said to be present throughout the process, for the absolute is at once what objectifies and what is objectified. Though an acting subject, this absolute is in one sense purely objective: it shares none of the limitations and contingencies of any specific human subject. In that Schelling's dialectic begins with this absolute and ends with the human individual, it is, in a very specific sense, a movement from the objective to the subjective. At the same time, however, Schelling insists that there can be movement within the system only because his absolute is a subject rather than a dead object.

The details of Schelling's early system need not be considered at this point,[5] but it is important to note that the mature Schelling viewed Hegel's logical onset as a misappropriation of the teaching through which he himself had surpassed Fichte. Hegel's *Logic* also purports to move from objective to subjective—from Objective Logic to Subjective Logic—but Hegel's beginning is with pure Being rather than with a subject, absolute or otherwise. In attempting to start with a lifeless objectivity, Hegel reverts, in Schelling's view, to the pre-Kantian standpoint of dogmatic metaphysical realism, and in completely excluding the subject from the point of onset, he unintentionally but unavoidably excludes it from the system as a whole (10:128–29).

The suppression of the subject not only limits the scope of Hegel's system; it also, Schelling continues, contributes to a misleading semblance of objective developmental necessity. The science must begin with some specific concept, and that concept must be selected by the logician. Since the system is to develop from the point of onset, the first concept must be one that can appear to effect a movement beyond itself:

> If the beginning were already completely sufficient, then it would already be the end. It must then be the most negative, and one must seek for the concept a beginning where it still has the least possible content. . . . Such a minimum of content is to be achieved, however, only through abstraction. This beginning is thus obviously, as such, a constructed one. . . . (*GPP*:92–93)

In that Hegel's beginning point is reached only by means of a process of abstraction initiated by a subject whose presence and influence remain unacknowledged, it is subjective in the pejorative sense: it is arbitrary. Its objectivity is trivial; it is by no means an objectivity that entails universal validity: "Hegel returns to the most negative that may be thought, to the concept in which there is least to be *known*, the one that, as he says, is as free as possible from every subjective determination and is, in this sense, the most objective" (10:129).

The illusion that the logician plays no central role in the *Logic* is further strengthened, according to Schelling, by a terminological stratagem that obscures his presence: "the *concept* is substituted for the thought, and the former is presented as self-moving, whereas the concept itself would lie wholly motionless were it not the concept of a thinking subject, that is, were it not thought" (10:132; cf. *GPP*:219). It is not nonsensical to speak of thought as self-moving, but to so characterize the concept is simply to abuse language (*GPP*:221; 10:138).

Hegel's most crippling presuppositions relate to the subject who thinks the *Logic*'s concepts and to the concrete entities from which the concepts are purportedly abstracted; these are not, however, the only presuppositions identified by Schelling. The discursive presentation of a doctrine of concepts presupposes, in addition to all the concepts that are to be systematically integrated, the laws of logic according to which and the copula through which the concepts are interrelated. Despite Hegel's claim to the contrary, then, a system of categories simply cannot be presuppositionless. Indeed, if Hegel's claim to presuppositionlessness were taken in the strongest sense, it would exclude the possibility of any system. The making of the claim itself

> presupposes the concept of presupposition, and as soon as [philosophy] says anything else, it utilizes language, which it therefore also presupposes. If it wanted to presuppose *nothing*, it would have to deduce language itself. For a philosophy presupposing simply *nothing*, nothing would be left save to confront all speech with silence. The most complete philosophy would be the most silent.

Recognition of the impossibility of avoiding presuppositions might lead one to conclude, despite Hegel, that "philosophy is the science that presupposes everything" (*GPP*:223).

In fact, Schelling recognizes that Hegel cannot intend that his claim of presuppositionlessness be taken as strongly as some of his formulations might seem to suggest (*GPP*:222), but Schelling makes no attempt to determine the true sense of the claim. Any adequate defense of Hegel must explain the system's presuppositionlessness; also defensible must be the function of the grounding conception of philosophy that leads or allows Hegel to begin within the realm of pure thought, and the status of the subject, the relation of the thinker to the thoughts. Such a defense would justify Hegel's presentation of the *Logic* as the first systematic science.

Speculative Logic as the First Science

Schelling insists that Hegel's beginning is crippled by unrecognized presuppositions, but in his critique, Schelling himself relies on questionable assumptions concerning the nature and structure of Hegel's system. Without offering supporting arguments, Schelling simply accepts the *Logic* as the first systematic science, and he takes Hegel's claim that the *Logic* is presuppositionless to demand that the science begin *ex nihilo*. These views are at best oversimplified: Hegel provides various preparatory arguments and explanations for the *Logic* that he does not consider to be "presuppositions." One of the introductory arguments, indeed, the *Phenomenology of Spirit* of 1807, was originally presented as the "first part" of the system, and though systematic priority was later accorded instead to the *Logic*, Hegel maintains that in one sense the *Logic* presupposes the *Phenomenology*, although in another sense the *Logic*'s onset is absolute, and as such presupposes nothing (*L*1:51–54/*SL*:67–70). Finally—in partial support of Schelling—the latter sense alone is visible in the outline of the entire system presented by Hegel in the *Encyclopedia of Philosophical Sciences*[6]; there, Hegel begins his systematic account with the Science of Logic, and suggests no reliance on the *Phenomenology*. Even there, however, he precedes his Logic with a fifty-page "Preconception (*Vorbegriff*)" which is acknowledged to be inferior, as an introduction, to the *Phenomenology* (*E*:§25A). Determination of the nature of this inferiority will begin to clarify the *Logic*'s "presuppositionlessness."

The "Preconception" is, according to Hegel, "disagreeable" as an introduction in that it is "merely historical and argumentative;" it is structured rhetorically rather than scientifically, it is intended to convince rather than to prove. Its function is to facilitate the reader's recognition that various questions concerning knowledge and faith that are often taken to be clear in and of themselves, and thus to be primary, are in fact dependent on the "*simple* determinations of thought" that are treated in the Logic (*E*:§25A).

Like the "Preconception," the *Phenomenology* is intended to prepare the reader for the *Logic*. It is, according to one of Hegel's descriptions, the "ladder" that allows natural consciousness—the human individual—to ascend to the "ether" of absolute knowledge, to attain the speculative standpoint from which alone the development of the system is intelligible. Some sort of ladder is necessary because the scientific standpoint appears to the undeveloped natural consciousness as simply perverse.[7] As an introduction, the *Phenomenology* differs from the "Preconception," and from the Prefaces and Introduction to the *Logic* itself, in terms of form: whereas the Preconception is "historical and argumentative," the *Phenomenology* is structured by the dialectical "method"—clarified in the *Logic*—common to all of Hegel's systematic sciences (*E*:§25A).[8] Though it may appear paradoxical, the *Phenomenology* is prescientific in that it is designed to *end* where the *Logic*—and thus the system—begins, but it is also scientific in that it is strictly dialectically structured. A brief consideration of its structure will reveal that the paradox is merely apparent.

The *Phenomenology* develops roughly as follows: the phenomenologist—the reader—begins by considering the simplest claim to knowledge that may be made by natural consciousness, that is, by the human subject. The most naive epistemological stance is presented as that of immediate sense certainty: the subject claims to be certain of, and thus to know, "this" which is "here, now." The claimed object is analyzed by the phenomenologist, and is thereby revealed to be something other than what the subject claimed to know. In the first instance, the subject claims to know the specific "this" which is "here, now," but he expresses the content of his knowledge by using the terms "this," "here," and "now," which are shown by the phenomenologist to be universals, applicable to different things, places, and times. The difference between the subject's claim and the true situation requires and thereby introduces a new stance of consciousness, one that takes into consideration the complexities that have revealed the previous stance as partial or inadequate.[9] The process continues until a stance is reached where the subject is confirmed by the phenomenologist to know what it claims to know; this is the stance of pure or absolute knowledge, where the subject is "no longer necessitated to go out beyond itself, and the concept corresponds to the object, the object to the concept (*PG*:69/*PS*:56–57)."

In the course of the *Phenomenology*, various world-views are analyzed. According to Hegel, the necessity of the development—in which the collapse of any perspective always identifies its successor—guarantees that all possible world-views are considered, in essence if not in all their concrete forms. With respect to absolute knowledge—or, as may equally well be said, knowledge of the absolute—the *Phenomenology* purports to refute three contemporary positions. Considered and rejected are (1) Kant's claim that the absolute is transcendent in that it is inaccessible to theoretical reason, and present to practical reason only as a demand; (2) Jacobi's claim that the absolute is immediately accessible through faith, but inaccessible to reason; and (3) Schelling's claim that the absolute is immanent to reason, but devoid of content. Important here is not the question of how, or whether, the claims are phenomenologically refuted, but rather the standpoint that results from that rejection. The subject at that standpoint is convinced—and, if the *Phenomenology* is fully consequent, *knows*—that the absolute is articulated, and that its articulations are accessible to thought that succeeds, in Aristotle's terms, in thinking itself.

The *Phenomenology* leads its reader to the standpoint from

which absolute knowledge is possible, but it does not include that knowledge; the account of the absolute itself is given in the *Logic* and developed in the systematic sciences of Nature and Spirit. In terms of form or method, the *Phenomenology* is as strictly "scientific" as are the encyclopedic sciences of Logic, Nature, and Spirit. Whereas the latter sciences are written for the subject who is already scientist, however, the *Phenomenology* is presented to the philosopher who has not yet reached the absolute standpoint.[10] The *Phenomenology* can therefore be at once, and without paradox, scientific and prescientific: it is the former because written by a sage—by one who has "completed philosophy"—and the latter because written for the philosopher, for one who still longs for wisdom. The content of the *Phenomenology*, the dialectic of world-views, is presented directly to the sage, rather than to the phenomenological philosopher, in the encyclopedic Philosophy of Spirit; the *Phenomenology* itself is not, strictly speaking, a part of the system.

The *Phenomenology* is one among many possible introductions to Hegel's system. It is the only one that is scientifically structured, and therefore the only one that provides presystematic *proof* that Hegel's standpoint of pure knowing is absolute.[11] This proof cannot, according to Hegel, be completely transparent in isolation from the *Logic*, for only there is dialectic fully explained. At the same time, Hegel insists that the *Phenomenology*'s development is visible, in itself, as necessary. Without the *Logic*'s aid, the phenomenologist may not fully understand *why* the stances of consciousness organize themselves as they do, but he must be able to see *that* they so organize themselves.

The *Phenomenology* and the *Logic* are thus symbiotically related: the relationship is mutually beneficial, but neither work is fully dependent on the other. The independence of the *Phenomenology* has been explained, and the necessity that the *Logic* be independent has been indicated: in one sense, its onset must be "presuppositionless." The autonomy of the *Logic* must now be considered.

The *Logic*, the science of pure thought, is presented as the absolute science, the ground of all truth. Since it is established as such

in advance only by the *Phenomenology*, there can be, independent of that work, no prior guarantee of the fundamental status
of the *Logic*. The fledgling logician who has not been phenomenologist can know the ether of pure thought only as the element in
which he has decided—for whatever reason—to live; he cannot
be sure that the development of pure thought will result in the
science that completes philosophy:

> If however no presupposition is to be made, if the beginning itself is to
> be taken as *immediate*, then it determines itself only as the beginning
> of logic, of thinking for itself. Present is only the resolution, which
> may also be considered as arbitrary, to consider *thinking as such.*
> Thus, the beginning must be the absolute or (here the same thing) the
> abstract beginning; as such it must *not presuppose anything*, it must
> not be mediated by anything, nor have a ground; rather, it itself is to
> ground the whole science (*L*1:54/SL:70).

The individual's decision to "consider thinking as such" is "arbitrary" in that, independent of the *Phenomenology*, the task of
thinking pure thought is not an absolutely compelling one. It is
one path that the philosopher may attempt to follow, but it has
no particular claim to being the *only* way that will lead to wisdom.[12] Pure Being—the *Logic*'s first moment—may function on
its own as the "beginning of logic, of thinking for itself," but it can
be confirmed as the beginning of the comprehensive philosophical science only when the systematic development has been completed. The logical onset is presuppositionless in that it is made
independently of any introductory argument that would influence the course of development. The beginning of the *Logic* is
not made *ex nihilo*, in that it is made only following the individual's decision to think pure thought, but neither the decision nor
the course of reflection that leads any individual to make it
functions as a question-begging presupposition, since neither af-
fects the logical movement itself. The start with Being is presuppositionless in this sense, and in this sense only: it is first in the
course of the logical thinking of pure concepts or determinations,
it presupposes no prior rules or determinations. That it in a sense
contains all within itself is not a presupposition in any pejorative

sense. Indeed, it follows necessarily from the emptiness of the thought that nothing is excluded from it. This weakest sense of "all-inclusiveness" is both sufficient and non-objectionable. All that is necessary for Being to serve as the starting point is that it be thought and, according to Hegel, only the reader who relies, in his attempt to think it, on illicit presuppositions will be hopelessly perplexed by the logical development. Hegel has completed philosophy only if that development is both intelligible and compelling. It is with it—and not with the *Phenomenology* or with any other introductory work—that Hegel's system stands or falls.

Response to Schelling

Schelling claims that the *Logic*'s beginning is relative rather than absolute in that it is conditioned in three ways: first, by Hegel's conviction that philosophy is a science of essences; second, by the unrecognized presence of the thinking subject; and third, by the experiential and intellectual capacities that underly the possibility of the thinking of the *Logic* as a human activity. The first of these objections has been shown to miss the mark in that it does not take into account the complexity of Hegel's beginning. Hegel admits that the beginning of the *Logic*, if made without the mediation of the *Phenomenology*, appears to be arbitrary, and has no immediately supportable claim to the status of ground of the one true philosophical system. Only as phenomenologically mediated does the logical beginning appear in advance as the only possible beginning for philosophy as science, and only with the return to the *Logic*'s beginning at the end of the circular system is pure Being finally confirmed as the starting point for the successfully comprehensive absolute science. The objection that Hegel's beginning is illicitly conditioned by a presupposition concerning the nature of philosophy is simply not justified.

Schelling's second complaint is that the thinking subject is necessarily present at the beginning of the *Logic*, but is ignored. Were Hegel's account metaphysically *realistic*, purporting to begin with an inanimate and indeterminate objectivity and to derive—or allow to emanate—therefrom a conscious subjectivity, then the *Logic* would indeed be a reversion to pre-Kantian dogmatism and would be vulnerable to the Fichtean–Schellingian argument that the subject cannot be conjured out of the object. The *Logic*, however, is anything but a derivation of thought from non-thought. It is, from first to last, within the element of thought: Hegel is an idealist. He differs from Fichte in denying that the science of pure thought is appropriately characterized as the science of the pure ego: "Ego"—or "subject"—as a determination presupposes its own distinction from the objective; it therefore cannot be the absolute starting point (*L*1:60–63/*SL*:75–78).

According to Hegel, "subject" cannot be the first pure thought, the first logical category, because it is intelligible only if "object" is already understood; the same sort of consideration reveals the impossibility of beginning with "object." At the same time, the *Logic*'s categories *are* thought by a subject. Schelling is thus correct in observing that the subject is present at the beginning of the *Logic*, but is ignored; Schelling is however wrong in believing that he has thereby located a logical defect. Since Hegel's beginning is a beginning, it is, taken alone, necessarily incomplete: no true beginning is fully intelligible in isolation from that of which it is the beginning. Because the beginning is not as such its own complete articulation, it *appears*, at first, "that thought is object for a (thus external) philosophizing subject." When the articulation is complete, Hegel insists, the apparent externality will have disappeared (*E*:§17). The subject is "present" at the beginning in that it is neither excluded from nor opposed to the emptiness of pure Being. The success of Hegel's *Logic* as science is completely dependent upon the capacity of thought to thematize its own essential content, in which it as thinker is included, without relying on extralogical experience. The subject will be thematized at that point in the development where it is dialectically demanded. It would be only following that point or, better, following the completion of the system, that objections could be raised. One could then try to argue, for example, that the subject had been thematically introduced only through an external reflection. But such an objection cannot with any critical legitimacy be raised at the beginning.

Hegel's beginning is compromised neither by his conception of philosophy nor by the presence of the subject. Still to be considered is Schelling's claim that the onset is compromised by certain capacities, experiences, or historical occurrences that are presupposed by the attempted thinking of Being. Hegel's claim that the decision to think pure thought is presuppositionless—in that the development of thought following the decision is not conditioned by whatever course of reflection led to the decision—has been generally explained and defended. Schelling objects, however, that any factical beginning in philosophy presupposes the ordinary experience upon which the philosopher reflects; thus, the factical beginning presupposes the "real world" of nature, and the subjective capacities of intuition, consciousness, and language. By the time any account is given, the rules of logical thinking must also be somehow present, and for Hegel's own logical onset with the thinking of Being, the determinations or categories that will be necessary for the project are also presupposed.

As is the case with respect to the thinking subject, Schelling has made an accurate observation, but once again, it is not clear that he has located a defect. Unquestionably, all reflective thought "presupposes" that on which it reflects and thus, to the extent that philosophical reflection is reflection on experience as a whole, it presupposes everything. While philosophical reflection is thus temporally posterior to sensible experience, however, its intent is to reveal the elements and capacities that make that experience possible, and that are thus, though temporally posterior, logically prior. That the forms of thought are presupposed by—as conditions of possibility for—experience of things is a point that the subject must, according to Hegel, have recognized before it can begin to philosophize on the speculative level (*L*2:225/ *SL*:587–88). Thus, although the point is confirmed and thereby truly established only within the *Logic* itself (*L*2:226/*SL*:588), it must nevertheless be somehow understood before speculative experience can begin. The point is argued scientifically in the *Phenomenology*, and nonscientifically in the Introduction to the *Encyclopedia*. Present purposes will best be served if the relation of philosophy to experience is described along the lines followed in the later, nonscientific account.

Philosophy may be preliminarily determined, according to Hegel, as "the consideration of objects in thought (*E*:§2)." The consideration or thinking of objects is distinguished from awareness of them through the forms of feeling, intuition, and representation, all of which are modes of awareness of individual things or events. Any tree that I see, any pain that I feel can be objectively situated in that both have distinct temporal locations, and the former a distinct spatial location as well. Thought, by contrast, is a mode of awareness of universals, of determinations common to various individuals: every time I am aware of seeing a tree, I use the concept "tree," and every time I am aware of pain as pain, I use the concept "pain." I use the concepts whether I focus on them or not.

It is because human subjects are first aware of objects as individuals that philosophy is possible only as reflection: ". . . because consciousness makes representations of objects temporally before it makes concepts of them, thinking spirit proceeds to thoughtful knowing and conceiving only through representing, by applying itself to representing" (*E*:§1). Concepts are thus in one sense developed from representations; this is the *only* sense visible from the prereflective standpoint. From that standpoint, all concepts appear to be derivative in that finite human beings can become aware of them only by abstracting them—often, it might appear, arbitrarily—from representations, intuitions, and feelings, which are free from subjective arbitration in that they are simply received by the passive sensibility of the subject.

That the prereflective standpoint is incapable of providing an explanation of the phenomenon of consciousness—and especially that of empirical knowledge—is the central contention of Kant, who argues, in the *Critique of Pure Reason*, that nothing can *enter* consciousness save that which has been *determined* by consciousness. Kant denies that our perception of externally existent things can be understood as a process in which generally veridical copies of the things are passively received: regardless of the impetus provided the subject from the side of the perceived object, the *subject* contributes to the perception both the forms of sensibility, which make the object accessible, and the conceptual forms, which alone make possible the integration of experience of the object into the unity of the subject's consciousness. Whereas, furthermore, such pre-Kantians as Descartes and Hume attempt to explain perception as a process in which sense data (impressions of colored shapes, specific sounds and so forth) are etched onto the blank slate of subjective consciousness, and then serve as raw material from which the subject, through syllogistic reasoning, constructs objects and their interrelationships, Kant insists first that the immediacy of our perceptions of *objects*—only reflection reveals that our senses can provide no more than sense data—proves that reasoning cannot be a part of the process, and second, that even awareness of the sense data is possible only if the data are *conceptually* determined by the subject.

Kant argues, then, that the perception and knowledge of real things—things that the subject does not create—are possible only through the involvement of factors that are subjective—which come from the side of the subject rather than from that of the thing—without thereby being arbitrary. This is true to such an extent that the subject can be aware only of what it spontaneously produces on the occasion of objective impetus. Realization that the subject does not create the object—which follows, for example, recognition that the subject can err—leads the philosopher to conclude that there must be such impetus, but also that there can be no awareness of either the impetus or its source in abstraction from all subjective factors. The Kantian view is so completely opposed to the naive notion that perception is purely passive-receptive that Kant compares it to the Copernican revolution in astronomy. What results from the revolution is *transcendental* philosophy, the study of the conditions of the possibility of experience, a study distinct both from the natural scientist's legitimate investigations of empirical things, and from the special metaphysician's illicit speculations concerning entities that cannot be experienced by human beings. While the transcendental standpoint may be opposed to the normal one (just as the heliocentric consideration of the solar system is opposed to the geocentric human viewpoint), it is, according to Kant, the sole standpoint from which philosophical knowledge is possible.[13]

The superficial "perversity" of the Kantian standpoint is retained by Hegel; it is this perversity that makes a ladder to the absolute standpoint necessary. At the same time, though the Kantian and Hegelian standpoints are similarly perverse when compared to that of naive consciousness, they are not simply identical. Kant, having established the ingredience of subjective factors in empirical knowledge, concentrates on how those factors can be understood as integrating with the impetus from the side of the object in such a way that sensible experience can result. Hegel maintains in opposition that it is not the functionality of conceptual forms in sensible experience that is of utmost philosophical importance; rather, he insists, it is the *forms themselves* that must be considered, for they constitute "*the living spirit of actuality*, and of the actual, only that is true which is *true because of the forms, through them and in them*" (*E*:§162A).

Hegel insists, then, that the conceptual forms to be considered in the *Logic* are presupposed by experience. In that they become visible only in the course of experience, however, it might appear that any account of forms is relative to the individual, who can include in the account only those concepts that have been important within the course of his own experience. The threat of relativity is avoided—the absolute logical independence of the categories from sensory experience as such can be established—only if, in the *Logic*, the categories are organized and determined, and even identified, not according to information directly provided through feeling and intuition, but rather through their own purely ideal interrelations: they must arise in the course of *speculative* experience, the experience of the thinker who thinks thought itself.

Hegel's claim is thus that the method of the *Logic*—a method grounded in the dialectical interrelations of the categories themselves—will allow the account to develop free of influence from his own contingent empirical experiences. The method is also to guarantee that the account is free of *historical* influences. Here, as in the case just considered, there is *prima facie* evidence that the *Logic* has specific presuppositions: the categories are won from empirical experience by a process of "translation" (*E*:§6) that has been the work of philosophy: "The history of philosophy is the history of the discovery of *thoughts* concerning the absolute, which is its object (*E*:10)," in the specific sense that "philosophy posits *thoughts, categories*, or, better, *concepts* in the place of representations" (*E*:§3A). Speculative science, the one true system as the exhibition of the necessary interconnections of all the pure concepts, is possible as a human enterprise only after the conceptual realm has been sufficiently articulated that its scope and content are visible—only, in other words, after the work of philosophy has been completed. Hegel owes his ability to identify the determinations that resolve contradictions that might at first appear to be ultimate *aporiai* to what he has learned from previous philosophers. Nevertheless, he denies both that he includes concepts in the *Logic* because they have been considered important in the past, and that he arranges the concepts that are included as he does because they have traditionally been so arranged; he rather insists that previous philosophers developed those of their doctrines that remain cogent from their partial visions of what he himself sees, and describes, clearly.

Hegel's claim, as of the beginning of the *Logic*, may now be summarized: (1) the entirety of intelligibility is articulated through pure thoughts or concepts; (2) the content of these pure thoughts is originally available to the human intellect in the obscuring forms of feeling, intuition, and representation, but none of these forms is able to explain its own content as determinate; (3) the freeing of the absolute content from its temporally original form is the task of a historical and individual process of translation;[14] (4) the absolute content, as dialectically presented following the complete translation, is visible in itself as internally and independently structured, and as grounding the intelligibility of feelings, representations, and intuitions. The objection may certainly be made that these assertions, made in isolation, are arbitrary; I have attempted to make them appear plausible, or at least intelligible, but they must be proved if they are to be of real philosophical importance. The final proof can however be nothing other than the system itself, the actual dialectic in its concrete development. Consequent criticism would have to claim either that at least some of the transitions within the system can be made only arbitrarily, or are dependent on experience and intuition (rather than on the contents won from them), or that the system finally fails to be comprehensive, so that there are important "contents," in no matter what form, that have not been included within the dialectical account. Schelling's further criticisms are of these sorts. They must now be considered.

THE LOGICAL BEGINNING

Schelling's Critique

Not all of Schelling's objections to Hegel's beginning are directed against the *Logic* simply as a science of concepts or essences. A second aspect of Schelling's attack focuses on Hegel's designation of the first thought as Being, and on his attempt to generate a movement from that initial category. Hegel's claim, restated neutrally (if thereby, for the moment, nearly unintelligibly), is that the logical beginning must be made with Being; that Being is Nothingness, and vice versa; and that the Being–Nothingness contradiction is sublated[15] in Becoming. Various possible meanings for these austere formulations are considered—and rejected—by Schelling; the defense of Hegel requires the determination of meanings that are unobjectionable.

The logical difficulties begin, according to Schelling, with Hegel's first category: pure, indeterminate Being cannot, he insists, be the beginning of anything for, as wholly indeterminate, it is a "non-thought" rather than a concept (*GPP*:224). "It is impossible to think *Being in general*, because there is no Being *in general*. . . . Being is necessarily and always determinate." More specifically, Being is always either objective or essential. The beginning cannot be made with objective Being, since the objective is necessarily posited by or opposed to the subject, to which it is therefore second. Thus, the "Being" of the first thought must be non-objective, purely essential, "with which nothing is posited save the mere subject." It is therefore an error to say that the start is made with a fully indeterminate Being. What can be thought as *first*, the *primum cogitabile*, cannot be pure Being, it must be "the subject of Being" (11:302), "Being determined as subject" (10:133), the "Being of the pure subject" (*GPP*:219). Visible in these formulations is Schelling's own conviction, introduced above, that philosophy must be grounded in the primal self-reflection of the pure—and thus absolute—subject; the objection relevant to the critique of Hegel's system is that pure Being, in Hegel's sense, simply cannot be thought. And while Hegel's own intention is to express the unintelligibility of indeterminate Being, it cannot be Hegel's intention, according to Schelling, to classify as a "non-thought" that which he has been so concerned to establish as the first thought (10:133).

Hegel's attempted move away from Being—the determination of Being as Nothingness—is potentially vulnerable to some of the Schellingian criticisms already introduced. Schelling has argued against the possibility of an objectively necessary dialectical development of pure concepts, and against the possibility of saying anything at all about a wholly indeterminate Being. Both the subjective arbitrariness of the development and the unintelligibility of the first concept are clearly present in Hegel's first move as it is interpreted by Schelling: "After I have posited pure Being, I look for something in it and find nothing. This is the sense of the proposition 'Pure Being is Nothingness' "(*GPP*:220). It cannot be the case that pure Being somehow becomes aware of itself as nothing (as a "movement of the Concept itself" might seem to require); rather, "*I* find it as Nothingness, and express this in the sentence: Pure Being is Nothingness" (10:134). Furthermore, my "discovery" is no real development, but rather a proof that the question has already been begged: "After I have posited pure Being, I look for something in it and find nothing, since I have already forbidden myself to find anything therein precisely in that I have posited it as pure Being, as merely Being in general" (10:133).

Schelling questions the meaning as well as the derivation of the Being–Nothingness identification. As is indicated above, he criticizes Hegel for introducing the copula without explaining what it means. According to Schelling, there are only two ways in which it can relate Being and Nothingness: the judgment is either a simple tautology, or it is a truly predicative statement. In the former case, "Being" and "Nothingness" would be simply two different expressions signifying one and the same content. The emptiness of the resulting identity-statement, "a mere combination of words," would rule out the possibility that other judgments or concepts could logically follow from it. Hegel thus cannot intend to present a mere tautology, and the statement must be intended to be a true judgment. The function of the copula in non-tautological judgments, according to Schelling, is one of grounding: the copula establishes the grammatical subject as the ground or bearer of the predicate. Hegel's first statement would then posit Being and Nothingness in the relation of potential ground to potentially grounded. If this were Hegel's intention, then a dialectical movement would be possible, roughly "in that one would allow pure Being to proceed out of the relation of subjectivity (of subjection), with the demand that it itself become something; it would thereby become unlike Nothingness, and would exclude Nothingness from itself, through which exclusion Nothingness would become, as excluded, in its own right *something*." Be that as it may, Hegel's dialectic does not proceed in this fashion, so "Being is Nothingness" must be, after all, a mere tautology. As a tautology, it is at least intelligible: "pure Being, since it is Being in general, is in any case immediately (outside of any mediation) non-Being and in this sense Nothingness." The statement, so taken, is innocuous in isolation. For Hegel, however, it is not an isolated one, but rather leads to Becoming (10:134).

The introduction of Becoming is the final point of attack in Schelling's critique of Hegel's onset. According to Schelling, Hegel can move from Being–Nothingness to Becoming only through the unjustified introduction of a qualification into the original identification: pure Being is "still" Nothingness. Pure Being is not said to be absolute Nothingness in the sense of the altogether–not of Parmenides; rather, it must be Nothingness in the specific and therefore determinate sense of not-yet-actual Being. Yet if this is the case, the Being of the beginning is not in fact indeterminate, but rather must have been already, if not admittedly, determined as potency (11:134–35).

The "Becoming" introduced through the artificial insertion of the qualifier "still" is, Schelling continues, itself defective as an expression of the movement. Hegel vaguely characterizes his Becoming as "the unity or unification of Being and Nothingness," but it is actually "the transition from Nothingness, from what is not yet Being, to actual Being" so that Becoming does not unify Being and Nothingness, but rather expresses the abandonment or disappearance of Nothingness (10:135).

"Becoming" is thus no more clear or distinct than "Being" and "Nothingness," and the emptiness of the propositions relating these concepts is such that they are not really subject to analysis, refutation, or contradiction. Once again, the problem lies not in these innocuous expressions, but in the fact that Hegel tries to use them as a basis for further progression:

> The Hegelian Concept is the Indian god Vishnu in his third incarnation, in which he sets himself against Mahabala, the gigantic prince of darkness (and at the same time the spirit of ignorance), who has attained a position of supreme mastery in all three worlds. Vishnu appears to Mahabala first in the form of a small, dwarflike Brahmin, and asks him for only three feet of land (the three concepts Being, Nothingness, and Becoming). Scarcely has the giant granted this when the dwarf assumes a tremendous form. With his first step he takes in the earth; with his second, heaven; and he is about to encompass hell with the third when Mahabala throws himself at Vishnu's feet and piously recognizes the power of the highest god. Vishnu then generously grants Mahabala mastery in the realm of darkness (only under his own supervision, of course) (10:144–45).

The analysis of Hegel's "Becoming" completes Schelling's critique of the *Logic*'s onset. The points to which the Hegelian must respond are: (1) that "pure Being" can serve as starting point only if it is *not* pure, that is, only if it is already determinate; (2) that to the extent that the identification of Being and Nothingness is possible at all, it is possible only through a *petitio principii*; and (3) that the temporary resolution of the first dialectical contradiction—the introduction of Becoming—fails to provide a basis for further development.

Being, Nothingness, Becoming

Speculative logical thinking—pure thinking—is thought think-ing itself by thinking its own essential determinations; this think-ing will of necessity, Hegel insists, be knowing, but at first, when the task has been posited but not yet begun, pure thinking "is without distinctions; this lack of distinction thus of itself ceases to be knowing, and only *simple immediacy* is present (*L*1:54/SL:69)." The *Phenomenology* shows—and the nonscien-tific introductions assert—that only self-knowledge, in Hegel's sense, can be absolute knowledge, but as of the beginning of the *Logic*, pure thinking cannot describe or determine itself as "knowing," since it does not yet know anything; no pure thoughts have been explicitly posited. As of the beginning, pure thinking has no determinate content, it is simply "there" or, as Hegel puts it, "only simple immediacy is present." Since thought, if it is to re-main pure, must think only itself, it must first think this "immedi-acy." This original content of pure thought must be characterized in such a way that no implicit articulation is presupposed; if there were such articulation, the beginning would not be a true begin-ning. For this reason, "immediacy" cannot serve as the first thought, because "simple immediacy . . . relates itself to its dis-tinction from the mediate (*L*1:54/SL:69)." The concept or de-termination "immediacy" involves the "mediacy" from which it is distinguished, and the negative relation of immediacy to medi-acy. As is indicated above, a similar consideration rules out Schelling's "subject" as the first thought. The only term that is suf-ficiently empty to serve as the beginning point is "pure Being" or, better, "nothing more than *Being* in general: Being, nothing else, without any further determination or content" (*L*1:54/SL:69).

Throughout the *Logic*, Hegel will have to provide names for thoughts whose contents have already been determined. The naming itself is to some extent arbitrary since, unless new words are invented, the names given to the pure thoughts will necessari-ly be ones used for other purposes in ordinary language. Hegel de-scribes the relation of philosophical to ordinary language late in the *Logic*:

> Philosophy has the right to take from the language of common life—
> which is made for the world of representations—such expressions as
> *seem to come close* to the determinations of the Concept. It cannot be
> a matter of proving, with respect to a word chosen from the language
> of common life, that it is connected with the same concepts in com-
> mon life with which it is philosophically connected, for common life
> has no concepts, but rather representations, and it is philosophy that
> comes to know the concept for that which [in common life] is mere
> representation. It must suffice for representation if, in its expressions
> that are used for philosophical determinations, it is vaguely aware of
> something like the same distinctions . . .

Many terms that in ordinary language are more or less synony-
mous, such as "being" and "existence," must also be used by the
philosopher, Hegel continues, to express subtle but necessary distinctions (*L*2:357–58/*SL*:708).

That the names for the pure thoughts must in most cases be selected from the words already available in a given language is not
of crucial logical importance, since the signification of each
thought must in every case be determined by the movement leading to it. The names of the pure thoughts are not destructively ambiguous in that the process of Hegel's *Logic* never requires that
either concepts or the names of concepts be analyzed in terms of
their various historical, philosophical, or colloquial significations. On the contrary, the difficulty of the *Logic* stems to a great
extent from the stringent requirement that only what is "present
at hand"—only what has been dialectically developed—be considered at any given point (see *E*:§19A). To be sure, "Being"
must be "thought," and from the totally empty thinking of Being,
an organic development to further determinations must issue; but
the development will be organic, according to Hegel, *only* if Being
is thought strictly and solely as presented, that is, as free of determination.

To think pure Being, wholly abstract and indeterminate, is not
to think *anything*; positively stated, the thought of pure Being as
such is necessarily, and at the same time, the thought of Nothingness. The pure Nothingness that is thus thought is not however
the absolute Nothingness of Parmenides, which may be neither

thought nor spoken. Rather, it is the Nothingness that explicates pure Being as indeterminate. As the explication of pure Being, Nothingness is not simply nothing, but it has no predicates or characteristics that could distinguish it from Being; pure Nothingness may therefore be explicated only as pure Being. To think Being is to think Nothingness, and vice versa. But with the description of the thinking of Being and Nothingness, more is present than simply these two thoughts: the thinking of Being and Nothingness is also a movement in thought, from Being to Nothingness and back again. If thought is to continue to think itself in a determinate and exhaustive manner, then this movement must be categorially specified: Hegel names it "Becoming." That this name is fully appropriate is clear from its own further determination. What is thought in "Becoming" is precisely the movement from Being to Nothingness and from Nothingness to Being. These two movements are distinct in terms of their directionality, and thus must be given categorially distinct determinations: they are specified as Corruption and Generation, as passing away and coming to be. In this case, the logical determinations of the concept "Becoming" are precisely those fundamental to the representation "becoming" in ordinary language.

The further movement of the *Logic* is considered below in relation to Hegel's method. At the moment, it may appear that the early moves provide very little basis for further development; but it is important to note that, be that as it may, the beginning of the movement is logically self-contained. It requires no appeal to anything like the specific experience of empirical genesis, to detailed knowledge of the *Phenomenology*, or to any other sort of external determination or arbitrary presupposition. At the same time, it may appear that the Being–Nothingness dialectic is simple wordplay with no real significance whatsoever. As Hegel is aware, his own formulations of the beginning run the same risk. The greater risk, however, the one that must be avoided at all costs if the endeavor is not to fail from the outset, is that of adding determinations to the first concepts in the attempt to make them more intelligible or imaginable. It might be said, for example, that Being is the category that excludes nothing—and therefore has no determinate content—whereas Nothingness is the category that excludes everything—and therefore has no determinate content. This reading suggests a sense in which Being is Nothingness and vice versa, but it does so only by assuming that Being and Nothingness are "categories" that can therefore "contain" certain "contents." Such an assumption, however, is as external as is that of Schelling, according to which "Being" signifies the absolute subject, which, prior to its self-reflection, does not yet exist. If in the course of the *Logic* we are never led to consider the logical nature of Being and Nothingness—or, to satisfy Schelling, the source of determination—then the development will have failed to be comprehensive; at the same time, if we had to have the formal-logical determinations at the very beginning, the development would have already failed to be presuppositionless.

Formal-logical anticipations are not the only external reflections that the speculative logician must avoid. With respect to the beginning, extralogical examples might also appear to be clarificatory. It might be noted, for example, that the relation of pure light to pure darkness is similar to that between Being and Nothingness: what is the same and what is different when we think Being as opposed to Nothingness is analogous to the sameness and difference of what we would see in a pure white light and in pitch blackness. This analogy relies upon sensible experience, and not upon the experience that is developing as a course of pure thought; as such, it is an external addition.

Neither empirical nor formal-logical reflections are necessary for the thinking of Being and Nothingness. Furthermore, it is not clear that they really facilitate the thinker's task. At most, they reassure fledgling speculative logicians that in thinking "Being–Nothingness" they are not doing something that makes absolutely no sense, or something of a sort that they could not conceive of doing in any other connection. Admittedly, Being and Nothingness make very little sense, especially taken in isolation; but they are, after all, only the beginning.

Response to Schelling

In criticizing the logical beginning, Schelling offers the Hegelian a choice: either Being is in fact determinate (as essential-objective Being, or as the true subject and substrate of Nothingness), or it is a non-thought. The Hegelian cannot accept the former since, as has been shown, Being is the logical point of beginning only if it is indeterminate; only in its indeterminacy is Being Nothingness. The latter option is more attractive; indeed, the appellation "non-thought" is not far from Hegel's own characterization of Being as "ineffable." Its distinction from Nothingness is, in one sense, "a mere opinion" (*E*:§87A; cf. *L*1:78–79/SL:92–93). Schelling's description unintentionally reiterates the truth of Being, but his merely external reflection does not recognize the possibility of further determination. In fact, Being and Nothingness are concretely distinguished, preliminarily, only through Becoming: prior to that the difference is ineffable. Only after the introduction of Becoming does the distinction cease to be a "mere opinion." Furthermore, with every logical development, the first two thoughts gain concrete significance: in the move to the *Logic*'s second book, for example, Being and Nothingness are revealed to be, and to "have been," mere appearances, and in the move to the third book, they are revealed as determinations of the Concept. Being is and remains indeterminate; only because the significance of the indeterminacy is far from immediately clear is logical movement possible.

Schelling offers the Hegelian a second choice, that between alternative interpretations of the relation of Being and Nothingness through the copula; the choice is between identity and predication. The Hegelian must deny that the two are mutually exclusive. The formal-logical classification of "Being is Nothingness" would, at this point, be the result of an external reflection. Judgmental forms, and the copula itself, are thematized in the *Logic* when they arise as dialectically necessary, when they are demanded as explications for immediately preceding steps. Yet even at the beginning, long before Hegel's treatment of the judgment, external (and thus inadequate) reflection on "Being is Nothingness" yields enough to indicate that Schelling's alternatives of identity and predication are to be rejected. In one sense, the statement is a simple tautology, in that there are no markers or predicates which distinguish Being from Nothingness, and thus, as Schelling admits, to think Being is to think Nothingness. At the same time, however, the characterization of Being as Nothingness is the result of the work of logical reflection which, at every stage, "finds deeper determinations" for what is posited in such a way that the determinations "are produced, but in a necessary rather than in a contingent manner (*E*:§87A)." In Kantian terms, the judgments in the *Logic* are both synthetic and a priori: they are known only through experience, but they are fully necessary in that the relevant experience is speculative logical experience, not the contingent sensory variety.

Independently of the precise meaning of the Being–Nothingness statement, Schelling argues that Being is reached only through an arbitrary process of abstraction that seeks the emptiest thought, and that only following this abstraction, and relative to it, is Being Nothingness. As has been shown, however, Being as first thought is not the result of an abstracting process; rather, "Being" is chosen as the most appropriate name for the simple content of pure thought before any specific thoughts have been thought. According to Hegel, other names could be suggested for this first thought, but analysis of them would reveal that, if their implicit contents were removed, there would remain no reason for using them. The only ground for preferring a term other than "Being" would be the content or signification of the alternate term, but the fact that the latter had a content would rule it out as the point of logical onset.

Being is Nothingness not because all content has been removed from it, but rather because the first thought, as first, can have no content; it is the "experience" of this thought—the speculative determination of it—that reveals it to be Nothingness. Thus, Schelling is in a sense correct in noting that Being is "still" Nothingness, but he is wrong in taking the qualification to imply "not yet (real) Being." We will come to know more and more about Being in that we will see it from an increasingly comprehensive perspective, in terms of an increasingly developed network, but "Being" itself will not develop, it will not "become." The logician does not observe the metaphysical evolution of—or emanation from—a primal entity; the logician thinks about determinations of thought, not about things either sensible or supersensible. The further progress of "thought thinking itself" must now be considered. It is not yet clear that thought can exhaustively think itself, but it should be clear that it can make a beginning in its attempt to do so.

2

The Development

SCHELLING'S CRITIQUE

The consideration of Schelling's objections to Hegel's beginning has revealed an uncertainty on Schelling's part concerning the nature of Hegel's project. Of various possible interpretations of Being, Nothingness, and Becoming, Schelling finds unobjectionable only one making Hegel's onset so indeterminate as to appear to be philosophically worthless, to be sterile and thus no true beginning. The account of the beginning given above indicates that Schelling is reasonably accurate in the description, but not in the evaluation. The fundamental error that Schelling makes there, and that he continues to make throughout his critique of the system, stems from his tendency to interpret Hegel in terms of what he himself takes to be philosophically valuable. The resulting divergence between Hegel's intentions and Schelling's understanding of those intentions becomes more visible as it increases in the critique of the *Logic*'s development.

The development of the *Logic*, if it is not to be in conflict with the demands that Hegel makes on philosophy as science, must take the form neither of an erratic and disordered gathering of concepts somehow available to it, nor of a sorting of concepts according to an ordering principle external to them. Either development would be systematically inadequate, in that either would rely upon unwarranted presuppositions, of content in the first case, of method in the second; and, furthermore, the result in either case would be at best a catalog of categories perhaps more extensive than the catalogs presented by Aristotle, Wolff, or Kant, but having no more claim to determinate completeness than would, for example, an alphabetically arranged presentation of the same categories. If the development of the *Logic* is to satisfy Hegel's own criteria, it must be orderly, and the order must be implicit in the concepts that are ordered. Differently stated: the *Logic* fails unless the categories are ordered in and of themselves, and in such a way that the order is accessible to the speculatively thinking philosopher.

Schelling attacks the *Logic*'s development not by claiming that it is unmethodical, but rather by arguing that it is dependent on a method that is illegitimately presupposed and externally applied. According to Schelling, the method is illicitly used by the philosophizing subject to guide the movement from the sterile thought of pure Being to a specific goal, which itself is arbitrary: just as the subject simply constructs the starting point, "the entire alleged process is constructed, and the self-movement is only a fiction intended to produce the illusion of an objective movement" (*GPP*:92–93). The subject, as motive force (10:138, *GPP*:221), determines the direction of development (*GPP*:221) toward a contingently chosen point of completion:

> That which silently guides the progression is always the *terminus ad quem*, the actual world that we have grasped, and Hegel's own philosophy shows how many sides of this actual world he, for example, has not grasped; contingency is thus not to be excluded from the progression, namely the contingency of the narrower or broader *individual* world view of the philosophizing subject. . . . the philosopher may try as hard as he will to conceal his consciousness [of the goal], but it will then work all the more decisively, as unconscious, on the course of the philosophizing (10:132).

Schelling's first objection is thus that the autonomy of the development is compromised by the illicit anticipation of a contingent goal.

As has been indicated, Schelling does not claim that Hegel proceeds unmethodically through the contents of the *Logic*. On the contrary, Schelling—who does not fail "to see the value of many uncommonly clever remarks, especially methodological ones, that are to be found in Hegel's *Logic*" (10:143)—is particularly anxious to have the method recognized: he claims it as his own most important contribution to philosophy. The originally Schellingian method is at once the "true essence" of German Idealistic philosophy (10:221) and "the only true discovery of post-Kantian philosophy" (11:334). Long before Hegel's systematic works began to appear, according to Schelling, he himself had applied the method in his *System of Transcendental Idealism* of 1800 (10:98), and had clearly described it in an article written in 1801 (10:147n2).

Assuming, in agreement with both Hegel and Schelling, that the method visible in the *Logic* is in one way or another "the sole true method," the important philosophical task is not that of determining which thinker was first to describe it, but rather that of determining who correctly uses it. Both Hegel and Schelling insist that the method is in no way independent of the content to which it applies; therefore, to the extent that the two determine philosophy's essential content differently, either their methods must differ, or the "same" method must be used in two different ways—which would mean, in the case of this method, that it would be misused by at least one of the philosophers.

Since the claim that Hegel misunderstands and consequently misapplies Schelling's method is central to the critique of the *Logic*'s development, Schelling's method must itself be briefly considered. In his accounts of his own attempts first to complete and then to surpass the teachings of Fichte, Schelling indicates what he takes to be the essence of his early method.

Fichte's greatness, according to Schelling, derives from his status as "the first to become completely emancipated from the merely natural form of knowledge, which Kant still retained as fundamental. . . . Fichte grasped the notion of a free science, to be produced through thought alone" (11:369). Fichte is said to have moved beyond the standpoint at which the subject takes itself to be intellectually dependent upon external objects. He thus moves beyond Kant who, in insisting that subjective receptivity in the form of sensible intuition is necessarily ingredient in all knowledge, remains bound to the "merely natural form of knowledge."

As has been shown with respect to Hegel, the first problem arising along with the project of a "free science, to be produced through thought alone" is that of determining the starting point. Fichte, according to Schelling, takes as his point of onset the ego, and he is not completely wrong in doing so, in that "in the ego, the principle of a necessary (substantial) movement is given, the ego does not stand still, but rather determines itself progressively." Hegel's Being, it will be remembered, is seen by Schelling as incapable of self-movement or self-determination, and thus as no true point of onset.

Fichte's error, in Schelling's view, results from his failure to recognize the motive powers inherent in the ego with which he starts. In Fichte's system,

> . . . it is not the ego that moves itself, but rather, everything is merely tacked onto the ego externally, by means of subjective reflection, the reflection of the philosopher, not by means of the internal evolution of the ego, thus not won through the movement of the object itself; and this subjective connection onto the principle comes about through an argumentation of such arbitrariness and contingency that, as has been said, it is difficult to find the thread that runs throughout (13:54; cf. *GPP*:177, 11:369).

Hegel's many "uncommonly clever methodological remarks" may seem to reveal the presence of a "thread" running through his system, but in fact his development is in a way more deficient than that of Fichte: the ego at least can be a true point of beginning, whereas pure Being cannot.

As is indicated above (p. 16), Schelling's development in the 1800 *System* begins with the primal self-objectification of the absolute. Schelling argues in addition that every subjective being—not only the absolute subject—originates in such a primal self-reflection and that, since this act generates a process fully determined by the act, the process must be fundamentally identical for all spiritual beings. Given these premises, it follows that if the philosopher can, on a reflective level beyond external influences, repeat the purely self-reflective act—if he can objectify his subjectivity as such, exclusive of the contingent contents of his empirical consciousness—he should generate, in his own consciousness, a process that will be an accurate imitation of the process through which the world itself, as grounded in the absolute subject, came to be. The philosopher will be able to test the accuracy of his reconstructed cosmos by comparing it to the world as experienced.[1]

A necessary movement is said to follow the primal reflection because "it is [the subject's] nature not to be able to be merely object, but to be at the same time, always and necessarily, subject." Because the subject is infinite, each self-objectification must be followed immediately by "a higher power of subjectivity"; for this reason, "with the first objectification the ground is laid for all following enhancements and thus for the movement itself." Roughly speaking: whereas Hegel first posits pure Being only to discover that he has posited Nothing, Schelling's infinite subject attempts to posit itself, but discovers that it has instead posited an object. Given an infinite and spontaneous subject whose "nature" it is to seek self-knowledge—knowledge of itself as subject rather than knowledge of any object—a move beyond the first self-objectification is unavoidable (10:100).

According to Schelling's retrospective summary of the 1800 *System*'s development, the first objectification of the subject is, as indeterminate, characterized as primordial matter. The subject, as now explicitly inclusive of this objectification, but as having no further content, reveals itself to be primordial light. The illumination makes the nature of matter more clearly visible, and it is appropriately redetermined, but that necessitates the rethinking of the subjective moment as well. The pulsation between subjective and objective moments continues through the "dynamic process" of magnetism, electricity, and chemistry—the basis of inorganic nature—and proceeds through organic nature finally to human consciousness and the adequate manifestation of the subject in the realms of religion, art, and philosophy (10:100–102). The "internal law" in accord with which the system develops is that "what at an early stage is subject, becomes object in the following stage" (*GPP*:194; cf. 10:104); that is, every self-determination of the subject is an objectification that reveals the subject only indirectly as the being that is capable of objectifying itself in the given manner. In this system, then, "it is not the philosophizing subject who moves, but the object moves itself according to a law internal to it" (*GPP*:194).

Schelling's method is thus no set of rules for procedure that may be applied at will to any and all subject matters, nor is it a method he "invented"; rather, it was "natural" to him (10:96). By this Schelling cannot mean that the method expresses his own idiosyncratic mental habits or tendencies. He must mean that he is particularly sensitive to the subtleties of the development following the primal self-reflection, and is thus enabled to observe and articulate that development.

It should now be clear that Hegel's use of method is quite different from that of Schelling. According to Schelling, since Hegel restricts himself to the ethereal realm of abstract logic—since he substitutes the concept, determined in the beginning as pure Being, for the absolute subject—he bars his access to principles that could generate a real development, and must simply appropriate Schelling's method, his "principle of movement . . . because without it he could not move from the spot" (10:212). As applied by Hegel, however, the method loses what guarantees its necessity, that is, the moving principle that develops itself. The principle no longer comes into play, and a crucial problem arises: "since mere thought is the vitalizing principle of Hegel's movement, what protection is there against mere arbitrariness, what keeps the philosopher from being satisfied with either a mere semblance of necessity or, conversely, with a mere semblance of conceptuality, in the subordination of concepts?" (10:138).

Schelling's claim is that the thinking of purely ideal determinations—as opposed to that of real principles that produce real things—has no necessary structure, that the logician is thus capable of producing any number of arbitrary phantasies. To be sure, it is possible to abstract various universal categories from representations of things as experienced, but since abstractions cannot precede that from which they are abstracted, the appropriate place within a comprehensive system for a catalog of categories would have to be following the explication of the origin of the human subject who is conscious of the categories (10:140). And even then, there is simply no unique order inherent in the pure thoughts themselves: "I believe myself that this so-called real logic could easily be done in ten different ways" (10:143).

It is worth noting that it was not Schelling's study of the *Logic* that originally led him to conclude that there can be no uniquely adequate "real logic." Schelling's "system of identity," developed before the *Logic* was written, provides a framework within which Hegel's system may be located. Viewed from the general standpoint of the system of identity, the *Logic* would have to appear to be either a science of ideas, or a mere science of concepts. If it could be accepted as the former, it would be philosophically crucial: for Schelling, the ideas share the infinitude and perfection of the absolute but also, through their mutual distinctness, serve as mediators in the movement from the absolute to the finite realm. Since however the ideas are absolute, Schelling concludes, in agreement with Kant, that they must be beyond negation, and therefore beyond discursive determination. This doctrine from the system of identity is presented by Schelling in his post-Hegelian lectures as supported by the Platonic–Aristotelian doctrine that the ideas are infallibly grasped through intellectual intuition. Embracing this doctrine, Schelling insists that there can be no mistakes with respect to the true ideas—they are grasped either fully adequately, or not at all—but that there can also be no science of them. The correctness guaranteed by the immediacy of intellectual intuition is lost, the possibility of error arises, as soon as the ideas are related to each other discursively: "The evidential rigor is there only when there is no relation among the thoughts (*keine symploke noematon*), but only the pure thoughts (*noemata*)" (11:325).

If there can be no discursive science of the ideas—the true *constitutiva* of things—then Hegel's *Logic* can be no more than a science of concepts. The latter are at the lowest stage of the Schellingian divided line. Highest is the absolute itself, the source of all being and thinking; it is followed by the ideas, for whose existence and content it is fully responsible. The third level is that of finite entities, including human beings, and the fourth, that of the concepts, which result only from arbitrary human reflection on the finite things human beings perceive. The concepts are not, in Schelling's view, veridically related to the ideas, and their "science" is of no philosophical importance.

Schelling does not choose to criticize specific moments within the development of Hegel's *Logic*; he is concerned with the system as a whole, and would see the indication of errors of detail as trivial and ineffective (11:42–43). He has argued that the development is guided by the illicit anticipation of a goal relative to Hegel as a human individual and thus arbitrary, that the contents of the *Logic* are arranged through application of a method that is entirely alien to them, and that there simply is no single order in which the fundamental logical categories—if it even makes sense to use "fundamental" here—must be presented. These are claims that must be countered if Hegel's development is to be defensible.

HEGELIAN DIALECTIC

Dialectic as Movement

If it is to satisfy Hegel's requirements, the course of development of the *Logic* must be dictated by the categories themselves. Hegel must thus have a "method" in the broadest sense, that is, his development must follow a continuous and coherent path; but this "method" must be fundamentally different from such methods as the experimental–scientific one, which purport to be independent of but applicable to any content that is of scientific interest.[2] Methods of the latter sort may be described reasonably completely in isolation from their specific applications. There can be, on the other hand, no adequate advance—or even retrospective—description of the path of the *Logic*. As of the beginning, the reader has only Hegel's assurance that the contents that are relevant will present themselves and indeed arrange themselves into a self-contained whole; the assertion can be adequately supported only by the success of the *Logic* itself. The reader who has been introduced to the *Logic* through the *Phenomenology* may find Hegel's claim more plausible, in that this reader has already—in principle—learned by phenomenological experience that the stances of consciousness arrange themselves "methodically." Even the phenomenologist, however, learns the logical truth only by experiencing the course of logical thought.

All that need be said, all that legitimately can be said about Hegel's "method" prior to the beginning of the *Logic*'s movement is that it is "consciousness of the form of the internal self-movement of the content" (*L*1:35/*SL*:53). "The nature of thought is itself the dialectic" (*E*:§11A). There is no access to this form except through logical movement. The content is the means to consciousness of the "method" or form, the method is not the means to the content—as Hegel himself stresses, in just these words, in response to the objection of a contemporary (*TW*11:417). For this reason, Hegel's account of the method can come only at the end of the *Logic*, not at the beginning.[3] The Absolute Idea, whose "form" is said to be the method, is visible only at the culmination: "the Idea is thought itself . . . as the self-determining totality of its own determinations and laws, which it gives to itself rather than having them already and finding them within itself" (*E*:§19A).

In fact, Hegel offers reflections and observations on the course of development at various points prior to its completion, frequently characterizing forms of negation and contradiction as they become visible. These accounts are not however intrinsic to the *Logic* as science. As Hegel stresses in the Preface to the *Logic*'s second edition, in the purest possible exhibition of the content no determinations or reflections would be presented that did not arise of necessity from preceding determinations. The practical difficulty prohibiting such an exhibition is that it would be extremely subject to misinterpretation. Human beings habitually think about things, not about thoughts, and the tendency to pollute the pure logical determinations with additions from the realms of sensation and understanding, as well as from the history of philosophy, would be for most unavoidable. For this reason, Hegel includes external reflections at various difficult points of the development, but these reflections are of a purely negative nature, intended to keep "unruly thinking" in line. These reflections themselves are contingent, and certainly do not rule out the possibility of misunderstandings. At the same time, Hegel sees them as necessary to counter the reader's tendency to commit the fundamental logical sin, that of "thinking, with respect to a category under consideration, *something else* and not the category itself" (*L*1:20/SL:41).

Hegel's extrascientific reflections on the development are thus included for pedagogical rather than for logical reasons. For the modern reader, however, they themselves can be quite misleading, primarily because they were intended for Hegel's contemporaries, whose difficulties may not always have been the same as those that face us. Particularly dangerous in this respect are the logical terms, such as "negation" and "contradiction," used by Hegel to describe the development. As Thomas Seebohm has pointed out, these terms as used by Hegel must be understood from within the context of a logic of *concepts*; the natural modern tendency to take them in their propositional-logical significations leads to tremendous and irrelevant difficulties.[4]

The peculiarities of Hegel's "method" that have been described should make it clear that the method is difficult to defend. As Hegel stresses again and again, the only justification for the development is the *Logic* itself, in its entirety. Furthermore, it is not clear that detection of flaws within the dialectic as presented by Hegel would or should indicate that the development is intrinsically defective. Hegel admits that his account is not fully adequate (*L*1:36/SL:54; *L*2:221–22/SL:576), but believes the flaws to be matters of detail that the careful reader will recognize as potentially (given time and effort) avoidable. Partly for this reason, Schelling does not consider details of the *Logic* in his critique (10:142–43). Fortunately, then, not all the movements of the *Logic* need be analyzed here. At the same time, however, the present need would not be satisfied by the interpretation, in isolation, of Hegel's retrospective presentation of the form of the dialectic from the standpoint of the Absolute Idea: the significance of the form can be apparent only to one who has some notion of the content. A minimal notion of the content may be communicated through an account of the division of the *Logic* into its three constitutive spheres—the Logics of Being, Essence, and the Concept

—the general scope of each of these spheres, and the necessity and coherence of the transitions among them.

Being, Essence, Concept

Hegel's *Logic* contains three books—the Logics of Being, Essence, and the Concept—each of which purports to be a self-completing circle. In the Logic of Being, each category that arises claims to express what its predecessor is, to determine it self-sufficiently. The later term takes the place of the earlier, which is therefore simply discarded. For this reason, Hegel retrospectively terms the process through which categories arise in the Logic of Being one of transition or going over (*Übergehen*) (see *E*:§240). Each determination of Being thus attempts to express what Being is: it is categorized as Nothing, then as Becoming, then as One, then Many, and so forth. The Logic of Being is completed when a category arises from which there can be no *transition* to a new determination. That final category is reached when it becomes clear that being itself can be determined neither as a multiplicity of finite beings nor as any characteristic of such beings. Being itself must then be free of all that differentiates finite beings from each other; it must, according to Hegel, be determined as Absolute Indifference. Since differentiation is thereby posited as present only on the level of the manifold beings, Absolute Indifference is fully indeterminate. If it were to be further characterized through a movement of transition, it could be determined only as the pure Being of the *Logic*'s beginning. This result closes the circle of the Logic of Being by confirming that there can be no further determinations of Being: further transitional movements would simply retrieve categories that have already arisen. The linear step from Absolute Indifference—the one that will determine it—must therefore be of a new sort if it is not to be pointless. Since Absolute Indifference has arisen as what is (1) not the finite beings either individually or in totality, but (2) nonetheless their being, it must, according to Hegel, be determined as Essence, the indeterminate source of determinacy.

The step to the Logic of Essence confirms the inadequacy of determinations simply of Being: no account containing only such determinations can be complete. This means, more concretely applied, that "what is" cannot be adequately thought *simply* as existing, that no manifold of distinct items or entities can be understood simply in terms of what the items and entities are: they can be, as manifold, only if they are individually self-identical and mutually distinct. All must be beings, but not all are the *same* being. If the account is to be complete, it must not ignore the ontological difference between the beings as individuals and the being that they share. The Logic of Being shows that items can be thematized as individuals only if they are all thought as sharing or revealing the same Being. Since the universal moment is unique—it is not itself a being like the others—it cannot be thematized within a Logic of Being.

Whereas in the Logic of Being, each category purports, as it arises, to self-sufficiently express the entire truth of Being, the categories in the Logic of Essence are, even as they arise, explicitly relative. Every category purporting to express the truth of Essence—such as Ground, Cause, Thing, and Substance—is unavoidably associated with a category purporting to express the nature of the determinate being of which the Essence is the source. Associated with the Essences listed above are, respectively, Grounded, Effect, Property, and Accident. Each time the Essential moment—Being as the source of beings—is redetermined, the Appearances—the determinate beings—are affected, and vice versa; for this reason, Hegel retrospectively characterizes the form of the progress through the Logic of Essence as one of *relativity*, in which the Essential moment "shines forth in, or with respect to the Being of," the moment of Appearance (*TW*17:408; cf. *E*:§240). The Logic of Essence is doomed to failure in that the source or Essence is irrevocably contradictory: it must be at once beyond all determination, and somehow responsible for and revealed in the determinate items of which it is the source. The dialectic reveals the inadequacy of each of the subtly distinguished Essential moments, and ends at the point where the unavoidable emptiness of the Essential moment is directly acknowledged. It is then clear that the items in a determinate manifold cannot be united, while retaining their distinctness, either in a being or in a hidden and indeterminate essence. In the transition from the Logic of Being to the Logic of Essence, the possibility of beings was posited in an Essence; in the transition to the Logic of the Concept, essences, appearances, and beings of all sorts are posited as grounded in a Universal in which they are united and conceptually interrelated. The Universal itself is Universal only in encompassing a manifold of Individuals through the Particularities in terms of which it interrelates them. In the move to the Logic of Essence, the beings are revealed to be mere appearances. In the move to the Logic of the Concept, essences, appearances, and beings are revealed to be conceptual moments that attain determinacy and distinctness only through their interrelationship in a conceptual whole.

The move to the Logic of the Concept is necessitated by the lack of any Essential moment that could characterize Absolute Reciprocity. Since the latter contains all determinacy within itself, a distinct Essence could be posited only as the fully indeterminate source of determination with which the *Logic*'s second book began; in that no new *relational* move is possible, the Logic of Essence is confirmed to be a complete and closed circle. This closing reveals that no manifold of determinate items can be understood in terms of its relation to an indeterminate or transdeterminate Essence that it purportedly reveals. The failure of the Logic of Essence thus indirectly reveals the inadequacy of transcendent metaphysical doctrines attempting to ground the factical world either in absolute entities whose absoluteness rules out the possibility of determination, or in inaccessible "things-in-themselves."

Since there can be no move from Absolute Reciprocity to any new determination of Being or Essence, if the dialectic is not simply to fail then the positing of Reciprocity as a *conceptual* totality must bring with it the possibility for a new form of dialectical movement. The moments necessary to this conceptual totality are, as indicated above, those of Universal, Particular, and Individual, and the three moments are inextricably interrelated. Since therefore the analysis of any one of the moments involves the development of the other two, the movement characteristic of the Logic of the Concept is characterized as one of *unfolding* or *un-*

winding (*Entwicklung*), wherein the thematizing of any moment explicitly leads to the unfolding of the determinations implicit in it. Furthermore, in that the move to the Logic of the Concept reveals that beings and essences are possible as such only insofar as they are so conceptually determined, it also becomes clear that the progress through the *Logic*'s first two books has in fact been a part of the unfolding of the Concept. It is only in the Logic of the Concept, then, that the movement of the *Logic* as a whole can be accurately characterized.

The first part of the Logic of the Concept, "Subjectivity," purports to establish the absoluteness of scope of conceptual determinations: in that even the negation of determinability, in the form of something like "the inconceivable," is itself a determination, it makes no sense to speak of a content to which no category is applicable. The same consideration that reveals the universal applicability of the categories reveals also, however, that they apply generally not to other categories, but to things that are not categories. This result leads to the book's second part, "Objectivity." Therein, when the importance of the determining subject's own ends to the precise determination of any manifold is thematized, a final turn is necessitated, the turn to the Idea. The Idea is the subject posited as constantly determining the object (objectivity as a whole), both theoretically and practically, but in such a way that the object remains object no matter how often or how completely it is redetermined. The subject is forced to acknowledge the impossibility of complete theoretical determination of what is (the impossibility that the Idea of the True be actualized) and of complete practical determination (the impossibility that the Idea of the Good be actualized). The final logical step is taken when the limitation that has been revealed is located in the object rather than in the subject: since the object can never, in principle, correspond to either the theoretical or the practical demands of reason, it is not worthy of those demands. In knowing that to be confronted with an objectivity at all is to be confronted with one that it has already determined, and that it can and will continue to redetermine (again, both theoretically and practically), the subject knows all that can be known about the essence of objectivity as such. This penetration of the essence of objectivity confirms the absoluteness of the Idea, which can then be posited directly in the ultimate category, the Absolute Idea.

The Absolute Idea is the subject determined as principle of determination. The content of the Idea is thus the categories in and through which determination of anything at all is achieved. These categories are however precisely the moments that have arisen in the course of the *Logic* itself. The Idea is not subject to further logical determination precisely because its complete determination has preceded it; it is for this reason that it can serve as the point of logical culmination.

Dialectic as Method and Standard

Hegel's anticipatory characterization of his "method" as "consciousness of the form of the internal self-movement of the content (*L*1:35/*SL*:53) should now be more intelligible. The German word here translated as "movement" is *Bewegung*, and the original term is significantly more expressive than the English one. *Bewegung* has as its root *Weg*, cognate with "way" as path or road. The contents of the *Logic bewegen sich*, they "move themselves" in that they give themselves a way. "Movement" is inadequate in that it does not suggest that the motion is directed or ordered in any "way" whatsoever, does not indicate that the Concept's self-movement is more than a chaotic agitation or excitation. The *Logic*, however, makes its own way. The speculative thinker in the process of determining the categories, as they arise, for the first time does not know where, if anywhere, he is headed. The *Logic* is possible, as presuppositionless, only because the determinations of the categories interrelate the categories in such a way that the logician need only pay careful attention in order to follow the development; he need not apply an external method. Thus, something like a "method" can be articulated only at the end. At that point, the "way" is known, the logician realizes that he has proceeded along a path—*met'-hodos*, literally, "with a road." When the course of the *Logic* returns the logician to the starting point, closing the circle, the logician truly knows that point for the first time, and knows also how it was reached.

The "method" described in Hegel's section on the Absolute Idea can be nothing more than an overview of the most general features of the *Logic*'s path—it can be nothing like a revelation, after the fact, of a concealed motor supposed to have been responsible for the movement all along. Throughout the *Logic*, external reflections may be made on the general form of the movement and on the architectonic; with the Idea, however, the task of reviewing the course of the path—now retrospectively visible in its entirety—and of thereby clarifying the architectonic is demanded by the course of speculative thought itself. Needless perhaps to say, the account does not determine the "method" in terms of extralogical categories. It rather stresses the moments in which the movement has become increasingly self-reflective, the categories that, with increasing adequacy, have determined the nature of categories as such, themselves included.

Pure thought begins by naming its original content "pure Being," but discovers in positing Being that the starting point is not simply immediate and indeterminate—or rather, that as simply immediate and indeterminate, it is not simply pure Being. From the standpoint of the Absolute Idea, it is clear that pure Being is in fact concrete totality, in that its development to the articulated totality of the Idea is logically necessary. At the beginning, however, the totality is only implicit; it has to be logically unwound. The logician's first step towards the unwinding is that of the naming and positing of the category that determines the first thought. Throughout the Logic of Being, the second category cannot be explicitly *related* to the first, since it purports simply to supplant it. Be that as it may, the thinking of the two determinations together leads to a specific sort of conflict. Once a certain level of complexity of thought has been developed—specifically, with the thematization of Contradiction in the Logic of Essence—the conflict itself is on the level of complexity of contradiction. Prior to that point, as for example with the Being–Nothingness conflict, the emptiness of the determinations rules out the possibility that the relation be characterized as contradictory. In the case of Being and Nothingness, even "conflict" is too complex. There, the recognition that a conflict has been thought is in and of itself the specification of the relationship as that of Becoming. In every case, indeed, the first two moments are redetermined through the category that names the conflict. The third moment—or, if the conflict itself is counted as a "moment," this would be the fourth[5]—grounds the determinacy of the first two. At the same time, however, since the third cannot ground if it remains indeterminate, it assumes the formal position of a first, it is as such opposed by a second, from which it differs in a specific way, and a new ground is required. The process continues to the point where, with the Absolute Idea, the second moment has *already* been determined, and thus *already* stands in an explicated relationship to the last thought. Beyond the Absolute Idea, then, progress is unnecessary and, in terms of pure speculative logic, impossible.

The form clarified as the method of the *Logic* also illuminates the architectonic: the sphere of Being as a whole is that of immediacy, where simple identity, or the individual, is taken as self-sufficient. With the recognition that it cannot be such, the move is made to the sphere of Essence, where difference, or the relation of one sort of particular (appearance) to another (essence) is taken to be crucial. Finally, when the closing of the circle of essential determinations reveals that every particular difference requires a new unity that can be neither being nor essence, the move is made to the Logic of the Concept, wherein is considered the articulated unity of the subject as the Universal that, in explicitly encompassing both the Particular and the Individual, is a true totality.

In the *Encyclopedia*'s treatment of the Absolute Idea, Hegel describes the method of speculative logic as "the determinate knowledge of the *Währung* of its moments (E:§237)." "*Währung*" is fundamentally economic in signification, meaning standard, value, or currency. Its use by Hegel here suggests that the methodical overview of the way taken by the *Logic* will reveal at once the nature of the categories as currency, their value, and also the standard backing them up, guaranteeing that they are as valuable as they are said to be. Hegel emphasizes three aspects of the dialectic that enable it to function as this *Währung*. (1) The beginning is immediate in that it is made with pure Being. From the standpoint of the Idea, it is clear that

Being is originally pre-supposed (*vorausgesetzt*) in the specific sense that it is, at the beginning, posited (*gesetzt*) ahead of itself (*voraus*); its explication is completed only with the Idea (*E:*§238). (2) The logical progression is free of nonspeculative influences. It is analytic in that "what is posited is only what is contained in the concept under consideration," but it remains a true progression by being synthetic, in that the determinations crucial to each category are at first merely implicit, they are "not yet posited" when the category arises (§ § 239, 239A). (3) Finally, the Logic is complete in that it ends with "the knowledge that the Idea is the one totality (§242)," and in that it is the Idea itself that knows itself as such (§243).

The presuppositionlessness of the Logic guarantees, at least in principle, the validity of the development for any intellect whatsoever; speculative logic explicates what the categories mean, not what a particular individual happens to think. The independence of the development from nonspeculative influences guarantees in addition that the categories are truly constitutive, that they are presupposed by experience rather than derived from it. (They are included in the *Logic* because they are intrinsically related to Being, the only possible starting point for a presuppositionless account of the constitutive categories, not because they have been considered to be important or useful by human beings.) Finally, the confirmation of the self-reflective totality of the Absolute Idea guarantees that further speculative-logical experience is in principle impossible.

As the overview of the *Logic* presented above indicates, the move to a new logical sphere always involves the redetermination of the nature of the moments constitutive of the previous sphere. The move to the Logic of Essence reveals that what had been determined as beings are more adequately thought as mere appearances, and the move to the Logic of the Concept reveals that the beings, appearances, and essences can be such only to the extent that they are so conceptually determined. With the move to the Idea, finally, the ability of concepts to determine objectivity is confirmed. Thus, while the speculative standpoint is reached only by those who have already realized that thought is ingredient in "reality"—that consciousness does not passively receive ready-made "things" that are somehow given to it (see *L*2:225/ SL:587–88) this conclusion is confirmed, and thus truly established, in the *Logic* itself, through the failure of the Logics of Being and Essence (*L*2:229/SL:591).

RESPONSE TO SCHELLING

The direct consideration of the *Logic*'s development provides grounds for the rejection of Schelling's critique; indeed, many facets of the attack have already been revealed to be inadequate or irrelevant. All that remains to be done in this respect is to note the specific ways in which Schelling's objections fail. Those objections, as presented above, concern the role played by the subject in guiding the development, especially through anticipation of the goal; the relation of the form of the development to the content; the possibility of a discursive interrelating of true "ideas"; and finally, the uniqueness of Hegel's as a speculative logic.

The status of the thinking subject within the *Logic* as present, albeit implicitly, from the beginning, and thus not magically added at the end, is described above in conjunction with the treatment of Hegel's beginning (pp. 24–25). As of the end of the *Logic*, the subject qua thinker of pure thoughts, the speculative or absolute subject, has been thematized and explicated. Within the Logic of Essence, it becomes clear that the fundamental problem of the *Logic*, as science of pure thought, is that of explaining determinacy and determination. The failure of the Logic of Being reveals that entities must be determinate, but that they cannot ground or explain their own determinacy; the failure of the Logic of Essence reveals that the problem cannot be solved through the introduction of an indeterminate source of determination. Within the Logic of the Concept, determinacy is shown to be dependent upon the subject who determines, and the *Logic* itself is revealed to be the science of the subject's functional determinations. The logical subject is precisely the Absolute Idea, as Universal in which all Particulars and Individuals are united. As such, it is itself Individual as the determinate negation of its moments; it is none in being all.

The finite human subject who decided to think pure thought is of course not purely and simply the Absolute Idea as it appears at the end of the *Logic*, but that is logically irrelevant. What the *Logic* tells the subject about itself is first that it is, as Absolute Idea, the principle of all determination, and second, that to whatever extent and in whatever way it is also a finite entity, its finitude will be intelligible only in and through the determinations of the Absolute Idea. The subject as finite, and the essential unity of finitude and infinitude in the concrete subject, are topics not excluded from Hegel's system; they are considered within the Philosophy of Spirit. The transition to the sciences of Nature and Spirit, and their status within the system, are considered below. What is important to note at this point is only that the subject is not conjured up at the end of the *Logic*—that its nature, as principle of determination, becomes increasingly clear through the course of the *Logic*. This establishes the ineffectiveness of Schelling's claim that the absence of the subject from the beginning together with its presence at the end proves that the development has been in at least this respect arbitrary.

Schelling argues not only that the introduction of the subject is arbitrary, but also that the development is structured by the illicit anticipation of the goal. It should now be clear, however, that the nature of Hegel's "goal" itself rules out the possibility that it is illicitly anticipated in the way Schelling imagines. What the *Logic* ends with is nothing like an account of the world as Hegel has experienced it; it is only indirectly an account of the world at all. To the extent that the *Logic* has a goal, it is that of determinately completing the experience of speculative thought. The individual thinker could be motivated only by the hope that that experience would be neither a chaotic rhapsody nor an endless monologue. That it is not chaotic is proved by the coherence of the linear development through the determinations; categories are not simply assimilated at random. Further, that the Absolute Idea is the completion of speculative logical experience is argued not on the basis of the claim that all available categories have been included—that Hegel could not think of anything else to add—but rather on that of the demonstration that any "further" movement would be mere repetition. In that the Absolute Idea is nothing other than the concrete totality of all that has preceded it in the genealogy of pure thought, it is not something that could serve as an ulterior motive for the development.[6]

The next point of Schelling's critique that must here be explicitly countered is the claim that the form of the *Logic* is external to the content, specifically, that the appearance of objective movement in the *Logic* results from the misapplication of Schelling's own method. That method, as described above, was one of an ideal dialectic—a movement in thought alone—purporting to imitate the real, cosmological dialectic, the process through which the world in fact came to be. The philosophically reconstructed world was to be confirmed as an accurate copy through its correspondence to the factical world. Hegel's dialectic, however, is ideal throughout, and does not claim to reconstruct a real process. It ends not with any world—experienced or ideal—but rather with the principle of determination, the Absolute Idea. There may well be specific structures within the *Logic* that are similar to structures in Schelling's works—as well as to structures described by other philosophers—but the presence of such similarities by no means proves that the structures have been illicitly appropriated. On the contrary, Hegel stresses that he is able to grasp the whole of the Absolute Idea only because previous thinkers had so clearly articulated so many of the parts.

Schelling does not identify specific crucial points at which he takes the method to be external to the content. Rather, his entire critique is based in the claim that pure thought is in itself unstructured, and that Hegel must therefore rely on an external principle in ordering his categories. As has been indicated, Schelling's claim is not a mere presupposition, it is rather a conclusion he reached through his own philosophical reflections prior to the appearance of Hegel's systematic works: those reflections led him to adopt the Greek doctrine that constitutive forms are known only through an ineffable intellectual intuition. Hegel himself does not deny that there is an "intuitive" moment in each dialectical move:

the logician must "see" the category that will meet the requirements of the dialectic at each point. Yet while the category must arise spontaneously—and thus be "immediate"—it is not known until it is analyzed, and thereby determined through its relation to other categories, by which it is mediated. Kant insists that awareness of real things is possible only through the involvement—in Hegelian terms, the mediation—of conceptual determinations. Hegel makes the same claim with respect to awareness of concepts themselves, and thereby insists that "there is nothing, neither in heaven nor in nature nor in spirit nor anywhere else, that does not contain immediacy as well as mediacy, so that these determinations are clearly inseparate and inseparable, and the opposition between them nugatory (*L*1:52/*SL*:68)." While awareness is immediate in that it does not follow any conscious course of reasoning, Hegel insists also that a condition of the possibility of the awareness of anything—any thing or any thought—*as* something, thus as determinate, is the tacit distinction of it from what it is not. For Hegel as for Spinoza, all determination is negation; for Hegel, all negation is relation, and thus, all intuition involves discursion. Conversely, since all determination is determination *of* something, discursion necessarily involves intuition: the two are "inseparate and inseparable, and the opposition between them"—a purported "opposition" allowing them to function independently—"nugatory." It is because intuition and discursion are as fully united on the speculative level as on the empirical that the judgments in the *Logic* can be at once synthetic and analytic (see p. 60 above).

Hegel's contention that a discursive science of constitutive forms is possible is further supported to the extent that the development of the *Logic* does appear to be necessary. That the necessity is due to the internality of the dialectical form to the categorial content is further evidenced by the fact that no one has ever succeeded in adequately formalizing that dialectic. Such a formalization is in principle impossible if Hegel is right in claiming that his speculative logic works only as a determination of its content. As is indicated above, the lack of a method generating the categories in independence from the categories themselves tends to confirm that Hegel is right rather than to indicate that he is wrong. Attempts to formalize Hegel's method such as, most recently, those of Dubarle and Seebohm, may be of interest to formal logicians, and may even be helpful to the reader of the *Logic*, but they are not directly relevant to the question of the internality of the form of the *Logic* to its content.[7]

The final point in Schelling's critique of the Hegelian development is the claim that Hegel's "absolute logic" is merely one among many. Schelling does not develop the claim, and the fact that no other such logics comparable in scope and rigor to Hegel's have been developed is *prima facie* evidence in Hegel's favor. Furthermore, the precise relevance of Schelling's imagined "ten different" accounts is not clear. If the "other" logics included concepts or relations unintelligible in Hegelian terms, then Hegel's *Logic* could be argued to fail to be categorially comprehensive, and the incorporations of the notions omitted by Hegel into other logical accounts would be irrelevant. If the claim were instead that Hegel's concepts could be organized in a different fashion characterized by an equally necessary dialectic, then the "concepts" would be the same in name only; they could not be the same in signification, since the significations of the *Logic*'s terms derive wholly from their interrelations.

If, finally, the claim were that the same concepts could be derived from a differently-determined starting point (one other than Being), then it would not be a criticism of Hegel in any serious sense. Hegel himself asserts that the *circularity* of the *Logic*, its systematic closedness, is ultimately of more importance than is the beginning with Being (*L*1:56/*SL*:71). Concerning the multiplicity of accounts, the Hegelian would insist that, for example, the attempt to start with the determination "Ground" would presuppose a complicated network of determinations such that, roughly, the Ground could be known in advance as the source of Consequences that depend upon it without making it dependent upon them—if it were *not* so determined, it would not deserve the name "Ground." The start could then be made with Ground, but since that is not the true logical starting point, its presuppositions would have to be unpacked before progress would be possible. Ground would have to be explicated as a certain sort of Essence, resulting from an attempt to understand the determinacy of Consequences, which are apparent, through a Ground that is accessible only through them. But this again presupposes that the consequences have already been understood as being apparently—and only apparently—independent and self-sufficient. The clarification of all these presuppositions would require, the Hegelian would argue, regression first to the most general sort of Essential relation, and to the nature of the defectiveness of the Consequences—which originally appear simply to be—that necessitates the search for their hidden Essence. This regression would require the determination of all of the categories in the Logics of Being and Essence that precede "Ground." Following the regressive analysis, the determination of Ground itself would have to proceed along the lines revealed in the *Logic*. Since there would remain the same relationships of logical priority and posteriority, determined through the distinction between progressive and regressive analyses, the categories constituting the Absolute Idea would remain genealogically rather than merely taxonomically related, and the "multiple" accounts would be ultimately identical. The claim that there could be many speculative logics gains its plausibility solely from the contention that Hegel's *Logic* can result only from the application of a contingent method to a pregiven content.[8] This is a contention that Schelling fails to establish.

3
The End

The Absolute Idea is a point of culmination, but the end of the *Logic* is not yet the end of the system purporting to complete philosophy. Just as, according to Hegel, the *Logic's* beginning is also an end—that of the *Phenomenology*—so must its end be a new beginning. Schelling is perhaps even less satisfied with the dual characterization of the *Logic's* end than with that of its beginning. He criticizes the beginning of movement from the Absolute Idea, the status of the Philosophies of Nature and Spirit (which follow the Science of Logic), and the relationship of the Absolute Idea to the Absolute Spirit with which the Philosophy of Spirit, and thus the system as a whole, culminates. The complex of potential problems is best revealed through a summary starting with what Schelling calls the Hegelian system's "peak of unintelligibility," the transition from the Science of Logic to the Philosophy of Nature (*GPP*:232).

Schelling first argues that there is no ground in the Idea qua Absolute for its own further development: "The Idea, at the end of the *Logic*, is subject and object, conscious of itself, as ideal also real; it therefore has no need to become real in a way other than that in which it already is real." Since the Idea purports to be complete in itself, the impetus to further systematic development must be external to it. Here again, Schelling sees the philosophizing subject as necessarily but covertly active. If the system is not complete with the *Logic*, this can only be "just because nature exists"

67

(10:152). The Idea as absolute, and thus complete, can have no notion of this nature, but "I, the philosopher, demand more in any case, because I am confronted with a real world and am determined to make this nature conceivable." The Idea cannot be conscious of any incompleteness on its part; the opposition between it, as ideal, and reality "exists only after an extralogical world is there" (*GPP*:226).

Schelling's argument on this point is based on the claim that the mediation between finite human ego and absolute logical subject is not yet complete as of the end of the *Logic*—the philosopher understands at best his own infinitude, but he cannot yet have comprehended the nature of his finitude—and that it is this opposition between unreconciled aspects of the subject, and *not* the Absolute Idea in and of itself, that leads to the Philosophy of Nature. Schelling does not deny that the subject has, as of the *Logic's* end, attained a sort of absoluteness:

> The Concept in its completion conceives its earlier moments within itself, and we can thus say: it is to this extent the Concept that conceives itself. But for whom is it this? For itself or for me? Manifestly, merely for the philosopher. It can also be said of the plant that it conceives itself in the flower or, better, in the fruit; but it is such only for the physiologist. If however this distinction is made, then not the Idea itself, but rather the one philosophizing is in power in the totality of the moments of the idea. . . . This [philosopher] could then be the Absolute . . .

If this is the case, the power is on the side of the subject, not on that of the wholly passive pure thoughts, and it is the subject, which has not yet grasped itself as finite, that breaks new ground following the completion of the *Logic*. Hegel conceals the fact that this must be the nature of the transition by always attributing the step to Nature to the Idea itself (*GPP*:231).

Schelling finds the defectiveness of the transition to Nature revealed in each of the expressions Hegel uses to describe it. The transition is announced on the penultimate page of the *Logic*, with the indication that "the Idea is still logical, it is still enclosed in pure thoughts (*L*2:505/*SL*:843)." Schelling comments:

After Hegel has assured [us] the whole time that the Idea is subject–object, the unity of the ideal and the real, the possibility that has its actuality immediately in itself, for which none of its actuality is lacking, —after he has said that the Idea is that whose nature can be conceived only as existing, considering which it is impossible to merely posit a reality for it—now it occurs to him, at the end of his logical ecstasy, that the Idea is still enclosed in the logical subject. Why?—Not through the Idea, since this was for him as Idea also the real, but because he sees nature before him, and cannot get around admitting that it is there. *The dialectical thread thus breaks off entirely*, and Hegel contents himself with being taught by experience that the Idea has been, so far, enclosed in subjectivity, that it was the mere Concept with which he had been concerning himself (*GPP*:228).

Hegel provides additional descriptions of the transition in the *Logic* and in the *Encyclopedia*:

The transition is . . . here to be grasped as follows: that the Idea free ly releases itself, absolutely sure of itself and resting in itself (*L*2:505/*SL*:843).
In accord with the absolute freedom of the Idea, it neither merely goes over into life, nor does it allow the latter to be its semblance, but rather, within its own absolute truth it resolves or decides (*entschliesst sich*) to freely release from itself the moment of its particularity or of its first determining or otherness, the immediate Idea as its reflection (*Wiederschein*) (*E*:§244).

Though the passage from the *Logic* characterizes the step to nature as a "transition" (*Übergehen*), Hegel stresses that it is not to be confused with the "transitions" to be found in the *Logic* itself. In the *Encyclopedia*, where the different forms of movement are terminologically distinguished, the move to Nature is contrasted to the "goings over" of the Logic of Being and to the relational steps in the Logic of Essence (Nature is no semblance, thus, no mere appearance). If, however, Nature is not to be taken as the Appearance of the Idea, Hegel's use of the term *Wiederschein*, a purely German word corresponding to the Latin-based *Reflexion*, is confusing: both *Reflexion* and *Schein* are thematized at the beginning of the Logic of Essence.

The technical classification of the move to Nature does not interest Schelling, but he objects strenuously to the description of it as "free":

> This absolute freedom can be thought only in this way: up to this point of its logical completion, the Idea or Concept was necessitated to move forward dialectically. To this extent, it was not free. Now that it is finished, it has nothing more to do. While it may not want to stand still, it is in any case not necessitated to move forward any more. Absolute freedom would, according to this expression, be nothing more than the absence of dialectical necessitation. But a mere not-being-necessitated is a far cry from a positively resolute freedom (*GPP*:226).

Criticism of the transition from Logic to Nature began to appear well before Hegel's death, and Hegel himself responded to some of it. In response to Franz Baader, who sees the transition as the "immediate issuance of matter from God," Hegel insists in the Preface to the *Encyclopedia's* second edition that he uses only categories in the *Logic*, and not images or "pictorial expressions" (*bildlicher Ausdrücke*) like Baader's "issuance" (*E*:17n). Schelling objects:

> At the same time, Hegel has the admirable category of release. This release is presumably no pictorial expression. What this release is really supposed to be is not explained. But this release on the part of God must necessarily be an issuance of that which is released (of that as which God releases himself), thus an issuance of nature, and therefore correspondent to matter and God; just as since, according to Hegel, God is in the *Logic* still enclosed in his eternity, he must then issue himself out of his eternity into actual, extralogical nature (13:121).

> This expression "release"—the Idea releases nature—belongs among the strangest and most ambiguous, and thus among the most timorous expressions behind which this philosophy retreats from troublesome problems (10:153).

Schelling's comments reveal his suspicion that Hegel's account of the transition from Logic to Nature is intended to be, in one way or another, an account of the creation of the universe. Credence is lent to this interpretation perhaps by some of Hegel's characterizations of the nature of the *Logic* as such. He says, for example, that the content of the *Logic* can be taken as "the exhibition of God as he is in his eternal essence before the creation of nature and a finite spirit (*L*1:51/SL:50)." Of course, Hegel never says that this is a necessary characterization, or even a fully adequate one, but in many places, especially in the *Encyclopedia*, he indicates that the *Logic* could be considered as presenting the complete definition of the Absolute or God.[1] At the same time, however, he even more frequently presents the *Logic* as the science of pure thoughts.[2]

The crucial question that is raised by Schelling's critique of the transition to Nature is that of the nature of the Absolute Idea as principle. The dialectic of the *Logic* itself is purely ideal; it takes place in thought alone. The question is whether Hegel intends that it become real with the Absolute Idea and with the transition to Nature. The *Logic* itself is in any case a work of transcendental ontology purporting to present the determinations that ground the determinacy of any thing that is or is thought. The Absolute Idea is thus at least intended to be an ontological principle guaranteeing the accuracy and adequacy of the categories presented in the *Logic*. If it is merely an ontological principle then, according to Schelling, the transition to Nature must be purely hypothetical: there could be a transition to the categorial/ontological consideration of something like "what nature must be if there is to be a nature at all" (13:89). According to Schelling, however, the expressions Hegel uses to characterize the transition argue against the ontological interpretation. "He uses expressions (such as 'the Idea resolves,' 'nature falls from the Idea') that either say nothing, or are intended to be explanatory, thus to include something real, an actual process, an occurrence" (13:88).

If Hegel's descriptions of the transition are at all appropriate, Schelling argues, the Absolute Idea must be intended to be a theological principle, an infinite God capable of creating a finite universe. The nature of the move from ontology to theology—from transcendental ideality to supersensible reality—if it is intended, is not clear, but Schelling seems to assume that Hegel relies on a variant of the traditional ontological proof of God's existence, according to which the thought of God somehow entails his existence. Hegel presents the Idea, according to Schelling, as "that whose nature can be conceived only as existing" (*GPP*:228). Furthermore, regardless of how the Idea might be established *to be* God, Schelling insists that Hegel's descriptions of the transition to Nature reveal that the Idea must be intended to *function as* God: the Idea as merely ontological principle could not be "free," it could not make "decisions," it could not "discover itself to be enclosed within subjectivity," it could have no "drive" (*L*2:505/SL:843) to move beyond the sphere of the *Logic*. Schelling concludes that the Absolute Idea must therefore be intended to be God.

Schelling does not directly attack the Hegelian version of the ontological proof that would have to ground the positing of the Idea as God; he focuses instead on the theological problems that arise if the Idea is so posited. The Idea is characterized as absolutely free, but once it makes the move to nature, "it gives itself over to a process from which it can no longer escape, against which it has no freedom, in which it is inextricably complicated. The God is not free from the world, but burdened with it" (10:159). God's free act of creation is "the tomb of his freedom; from now on he is in a process or is himself process; he is admittedly not the God who has nothing to do . . . , he is instead the God of eternal, continual doing, of unceasing unrest, who finds no Sabbath . . ." (10:160). Since the development through the Philosophy of Nature is necessary, a movement from moment to moment and from sphere to sphere, God's "life is a circular course of figures (*Gestalten*), in that he continually expresses himself, in order to return to himself, and always returns to himself in order once again to express himself" (10:160).

Even if it is the case, however, that the Absolute Idea is intended to be a theological principle and the transition to Nature something like a creation, so that the "real world" is intended to be derived, as real, within Hegel's system, even then, according to

Schelling, Hegel's reality is finally revealed to be illusory in that, at the end of the *Encyclopedia*—at the end of the system—the Absolute Idea in its eternal, ideal form once again appears as the culmination, in such a way that the reality of Nature and finite Spirit is ultimately denied: "In the last Idea, the entirety of the actual process is sublated, and the Idealism, in the last moment, falls manifestly and unashamedly back into a subjective Idealism" (*GPP*:234). "In the last thought, all temporality is explained away as sublated. Everything sinks into a colorless nothingness" (*GPP*:236). Hegel thus, according to Schelling, never gets to Nature and Spirit as aspects of an actually existent world; for Hegel, rather, "Nature can only contain what was already in the Idea ... the system is a Wolffianism raised to a higher power" (*GPP*:225). As metaphysical, the system is defective from beginning to end; in teaching that all is the Idea, Hegel produces a form of pantheism,

> but not the pure, peaceful pantheism of Spinoza, in which the things are pure logical emanations of the divine nature; this is given up for the sake of the introduction of a system of divine activity and effectiveness in which, however, the divine freedom is lost all the more disgracefully in that there is the illusion that the attempt has been made to preserve and honestly retain it. The region of pure rational science is forsaken, for [Hegel's creation] is freely resolved, it is the act that absolutely interrupts the merely logical succession, and yet even this freedom appears again as merely illusory in that one sees oneself forced, in the end, towards that thought that once again sublates everything that has occurred, everything historical; because one must come to one's senses and return to the purely rational (10:159).

The points made in Schelling's critique of the transition to Nature may now be summarized. (1) Whether the Absolute Idea is intended to be a theological or an ontological principle, it is complete as of the end of the *Logic*, and the impetus for the move to Nature must therefore be external. (2) Nothing in the *Logic* establishes the Idea as God, but Hegel's characterizations of the transition to Nature indicate that the Idea must be God, in that it is given properties that could belong only to a real being. (3) If the

Idea is supposed to be God, then its relation to the finite realm—
Nature and Spirit—is defective in two ways, namely (a) after the
transition, it appears to be subordinated to the real process that it
has inaugurated, and seems thereby to have negated its own purportedly absolute freedom; (b) after the description of the process
is concluded, the reality of time, nature, and finite spirit is again
denied, and the Idea loses its character as a supersensible entity
—it becomes clear at the end that the entire process has been accomplished in thought alone, that the dialectic has been ideal
rather than real throughout the system.

The interpretation of the *Logic* that has developed in the present study through the defense of Hegel from other aspects of
Schelling's critique unequivocally supports Schelling's contention
that the *Logic* cannot establish a theological principle: its dialectic is purely ideal, and does not derive, or attempt to derive, an existent God. Furthermore, it must be acknowledged that Hegel's
treatment of the Absolute Idea provides nothing like an adequate
creation doctrine. *If* Hegel's first philosophy is taken to be metaphysical theology, then his system is completely vulnerable to
Schelling's critique—or, indeed, to his *own* critique, in the Logic
of Essence, of teachings based in transcendent metaphysical
grounds. *If* Hegel's system can be grounded only in a supersensible entity, then it represents only a turning point in the history of
ideas; it can have no defensible claim to being the completion of
philosophy in wisdom. It can make this claim only if it is interpreted as transcendental ontology. The dialectic must continue to
be ideal throughout the realms of Nature and Spirit, it must not be
taken to become an account of the emanation of beings. The serious question is not whether Hegel intended to be a theologian or
an ontologist, but rather of the possibility and significance of Philosophies of Nature and Spirit within a system that continues to
be ontological. Essential to the answering of the question is a
closer consideration of the Absolute Idea as the system's principle.

THE ABSOLUTE IDEA

The Absolute Idea as Principle

The Absolute Idea is "the absolute truth, all truth" (*E*:§236), "truth that knows itself, all truth" (*L*2:484/SL:843). There are various senses in which the Idea is true, and these must be distinguished. First and most clearly, the Absolute Idea is true in itself in a way in which no preceding logical moment has been. At every earlier stage, the full determination of any moment reveals it to be different from that as which it arises: Entity, for example, arises as the thought of a stable, self-sufficient being, but further determination reveals that any Entity is thinkable only as one among many; Cause arises as that from which an Effect issues, and only its determination reveals that it is dependent on its Effect, in that it is a Cause only to the extent that it functions as such. The Absolute Idea, and it alone, is thought as the complex totality of all the logical moments; since the attempt at further logical determination of the Idea would result only in reiteration, the completeness of the Idea's determination is confirmed. In that the Idea is precisely what it has been determined to be, it is true.

The Absolute Idea is true also in that it grounds the truth of all the logical moments, in its function as their *Währung*. As the examination of Hegel's method indicates, each logical moment is originally determined through its relations to its opposite and to the ground in which it and its opposite are united, but the determination is not complete until the ground itself is determined in similar fashion; it is the necessity of determining each ground-moment as it arises that keeps the dialectic going. Ultimately, the logical dialectic comes to its end with the Absolute Idea. The latter, as fully articulated whole, grounds all the logical moments as interrelated in a fully determinate and specified manner. It is only as a moment of the Absolute Idea that any preceding determination can be true.

The Absolute Idea is thus itself true, and it grounds the truth of the logical categories; as such, it is the highest truth of the speculative realm, but its relevance to the finite, empirical realm has not yet been directly indicated. It might appear that the "real world" is composed of things rather than thoughts, and that it is the thing that is the source or locus of truth for the proposition or judgment referring to it. Hegel, following Kant, disagrees, insisting that there is nothing to say about what things might be like independent of the subject:

The object as it is without thought and the concept is a representation or a name; it is in the determinations of thought and of the concept that it is what it is. In fact, [these determinations] are all that are really important (*kommt es daher auf sie allein an*); they are the true object and content of reason and what is generally taken, in distinction from them, to be object and content, is valid only (*gilt nur*) in and through them (*L*2:493-94/SL:833).

Hegel contends that the determinations of thought—thus, the Absolute Idea—ground truth in the real as well as in the ideal realm. The Absolute Idea purports to be the absolute ontological principle, encompassing the fundamental categories in and through which alone anything at all can be determinate. The status of the Idea as *ontological* principle will be clarified by a brief reconsideration of the general nature of ontology.

Wolff's ontology—his *metaphysica generalis*—is a science of categories rather than of things: it presents and describes the concepts or predicates that distinguish things from one another and relate them to one another. The categories become doctrinally crucial when used in *metaphysica specialis* to determine supersensible entities, such as God and the soul. Purported ontological connections allow the Wolffian metaphysician to conclude, for example, that since God is perfect he must exist (existence being a necessary attribute of the perfect), and that since the soul is not composite, it must be indestructible.

Wolff's assumption that the simple application of ontological categories to supersensible objects would yield knowledge of transcendent entities is, as is indicated above in the Introduction, threatened by empiricists, and sharply attacked by Kant in the *Critique of Pure Reason*. Kant does not object to Wolff's categorial determinations as such; indeed, he praises Wolff for the clarity of his presentation of the fundamental distinctions, and denies the possibility of the significant extension of the scope of Aristotelian ontology.[3] At the same time, however, Kant insists that Wolff's ontology is defective in that it lacks an adequate deduction of the categories. Since Wolff merely assembles the categories generally used by philosophers, he can offer no proof that his list is complete. Since he does not derive his categories *a priori*, his ontology is also vulnerable to the empiricist claim that the categories result from an arbitrary process of abstraction from objects given in sensible experience.

Kant's solution to the deduction problem is such that, if accepted, it serves both to establish the *a priori* validity of the categories in sensible experience, and to limit the applicability of the categories to such experience. In opposition to the empiricists, Kant argues that experience cannot result from simple sensory givenness: experience requires assimilation into a unitary stream of consciousness. Kant grants that the empiricists are right in asserting that some concepts are empirical, and that such concepts are abstracted from specific experiences and then arbitrarily, and often illicitly, applied to others; but Kant denies that this can be true of all concepts. The problem becomes that of distinguishing categories—the truly constitutive, *a priori* concepts—from empirical concepts. Kant argues that since experience is made possible by the unification or synthesis, in and by consciousness, of the sensibly given manifold, the categories must be the fundamental forms of synthesis. These forms are neither abstracted from nor applied to objects, because independent of the forms there are no objects. Sensory experience requires some non-subjective impetus—often termed by Kant a given manifold—but there can be no awareness of this impetus in its pure state: consciousness of it is possible only through categorial determination. The categories, as conditions of the possibility of experience, are as such conditions of the possibility of objects of experience (see A158/B197).

The fundamental synthetic forms are, according to Kant, visible in the judgmental forms identified by formal logic. Once the judgmental forms have been identified—as they were as early as the time of Aristotle (Bviii)—their tranformation into pure categorial form presents, according to Kant, no problems. The presence of the categories in the judgmental forms answers the first question that must be asked of any deduction of categories, the question of fact (*quaestio facti*): it shows that Kant's categories are the ones we in fact use. The necessity of the categories for experience answers the second essential question, the question of right (*quaestio juris*): it shows that we are justified in structuring experience through the categories, in that there is simply no way in which consciousness of objects, or of anything else, could arise without them.

Kant's categories are, then, the forms that make possible the synthesis of a sensibly given manifold. As such, however, they are constitutive only of objects of sensory experience, and Wolff's application of them to supersensible entities is an unjustifiable extension. Kant's transcendental grounding of theoretical knowledge in the empirical realm—intended to overcome the empiricist claim that all knowledge is *a posteriori*—is thus at the same time a denial of theoretical access to the objects of interest to the special metaphysician. For Kant, there is access to God and the soul only for practical reason.

As Kantian transcendental logic, ontology is the science of the conditions of possibility of empirical knowledge, of knowledge of objects. Kant however remains silent concerning the conditions of possibility of transcendental knowledge, that is, of knowledge of categories and, generally, of the transcendental grounds of experience. In the view of the later German Idealists, it is because Kant is concerned with only a certain sort of knowledge that he can take synthesis to be the fundamental function of constitutive consciousness. Indeed, according to those who follow, Kant's notion of a synthesis of a "given manifold" is already nonsensical: "synthesis" presupposes determinate items to be synthesized, yet according to Kant himself determinate items are themselves possible only as syntheses.[4] And even if Kant's "manifold" could be given an interpretation sufficiently loose as to be nonobjectionable, it would remain the case that synthesis of a sensibly given manifold cannot suffice to explain or ground transcendental knowledge.[5]

As the account of Hegel's *Logic* given above indicates, it is Hegel's contention that determination, not synthesis, is the fundamental function of consciousness. If this is the case, then the content of ontology will not be merely synthetic functions, it will instead include all of consciousness's determinative functions. As has also been shown, Hegel asserts that these determinations—

the categories of his ontology—can be identified and determined through speculative logic.

Hegel's deduction of categories purports, further, to solve a fundamental ontological problem not directly considered by Kant: the problem of the ultimate grounding of the determinacy of the categories themselves. The classical "solution" to this problem—that adopted first by both Plato and Aristotle—is based on the claim that there must be a privileged evidential access to the highest genera, that the hightest concepts are determinately known, individually, through an intellectual intuition. Hegel, more radical even than Kant in his critique of intuitive givenness, denies that this is a real explanation. Regardless of the source of any sort of content, Hegel argues, we are aware of the content as determinate—it is more than a "mere name" —only insofar as it is discursively, thus categorially, determined:

> [The judgment] has as its subject . . . something immediate, any being at all, but as its predicate—as that which is to express what the subject is—a universal, the thought; the judgment itself thus has the sense: *the being is not a being, but a thought* (*TW*17:441; cf. 445).

This is not to say that the "being" is purely a product of the subject's constitutive activity (*TW*17:445). Hegel's intent is rather to stress that there can be no purely given "objective" being about which the subject could then think; rather, the subject has already played a crucial role in constituting anything thematized in consciousness, anything about which it thinks. Even the simplest of sensory qualities is by no means "immediately given" as such: there can be no awareness of, for example, redness independent of awareness of other colors that red is not, and to which redness stands in relations that may be—and indeed are, at least implicitly—categorially determined.

> In saying "quality," I express simple determinateness; it is through quality that one entity (*Dasein*) is distinguished from another, or is an entity; it is for itself—it subsists—through this self-singleness. But it is thereby essentially thought.—This shows that being is thinking; this is the insight that tends to be missed by ordinary nonconceptual talk of the identity of thinking and being (*PG*:45/*PS*:33)

Insight into the identity of being and thinking is taken by metaphysical cosmologists to indicate that thinking arises or emanates from a primal absolute object, and by metaphysical theologians to reveal that being is created by a primal absolute subject. For Hegel, however, being and thinking are the same in that thinking is already ingredient in any being of which there is any awareness whatsoever. The categories necessary to thought as such are therefore valid for any and all intellectual content, and the science of them can claim to be the fundamental science—first philosophy—without positing the existence of entities either sensible or supersensible. The special metaphysician asserts that the absolute must be both real and ideal ground, that it must ground the being of what is as well as consciousness of it. Those who take the absolute to be an existent object advocate doctrines of transcendent realism; those who take it to be an existent subject, doctrines of transcendent idealism. The transcendental or ontological idealist insists that, regardless of the nature or accessibility of the real ground, the ideal ground is both accessible and explicable. Though some of Hegel's locutions suggest that he is concerned with the real ground, and thus with a transcendent, theological idealism, he presents no arguments that could estabish the Idea as God. If his first philosophy is transcendent metaphysics, then it is dogmatic. Only as transcendental ontology can the *Logic* function as first philosophy.

Hegel insists that the task of first philosophy is the presentation of the necessary categories in their determinacy, and he insists that that determinacy cannot be understood as resulting from any simple givenness. If, however, determination cannot be grounded in a non-sensory categorial intuition whose content would remain to an extent ineffable, then the problem demands a discursive solution. The straightforward attempt—that attributed by Hegel to the "thinking of the understanding"—requires grounding in a single highest category, the *summum genus*. The impossibility of such grounding is, however, clear already to Aristotle. Plato, in the *Sophist*, examines the possibility of grounding determination in a *symploke* or network of highest genera, such that each grounding moment is determined through its relation to other such moments. Plato does not however attempt to complete the *symploke* and, in the *Parmenides*, he presents Socrates as driven to confusion by the contradictions that arise when the highest categories are interrelated.

Even if Plato was halted by categorial contradictions, the Hegelian would argue, he was nonetheless looking in the right direction. As the Logic of Essence reveals, there is necessarily a point in the movement toward the Absolute Idea where it appears that "everything is contradictory," and thus that all is indeterminate (*L*2:58/SL:39). Given this appearance, there are two intellectual options, two ways to attempt to avoid acknowledging that all is contradictory. Reason analyzes specific contradictions as they arise, it searches for the grounds that will resolve them, and its efforts are ultimately rewarded when it reaches the true ground, the Absolute Idea. Reason thus continually goes *zum Grunde*—toward the true ground—and the contradictions are thereby overcome (*ausgelöst*) one by one. The second intellectual option is that of the understanding, which sees the contradictions as threatening all that it has held to be true. Rather than risking losing its convictions, the understanding clings dogmatically to its presuppositions, refusing to examine them; it thereby goes *Zugrunde*—it is ruined, destroyed—in that it has failed to ground, and thus truly to understand, anything at all (*L*2:51-52,62/SL:434-35,443).

In presenting the categorial *symploke* of the Absolute Idea, Hegel claims to overcome all the defects of dogmatic and of Kantian ontology. First, with respect to completeness, the categories are not merely presupposed as given, but are rather progressively derived by speculative logical thought; the thoughts are included in the *Logic* because they arise in the course of speculative experience, not because they are visible in empirical experience. The completeness of the account is guaranteed not by any externally demonstrable comprehensiveness, but rather by its circularity, and by the architectonic, which reveals the insufficiency of the relations of transition and relativity, and then the absoluteness of the conceptual relation. Furthermore, Hegel claims to present the categories fundamental to *all* thought as determinate, not merely those necessary for the thought of perceived objects. Unlike Kant, then, he systematically relates the objective categories and the concepts of reflection, thereby grounding transcendental as well as empirical thought.

Hegel's speculative logic, unlike Wolff's dogmatic ontology, can also claim to be unique, not opposable by others having the same status. The development of the categories in the process of thought thinking itself, in isolation from non-speculative influences, purports to guarantee the status of the *Logic's* determinations as those essential to any thought whatsoever, not merely to the thought of the human intellect. Finally, the complete interrelatedness of the logical determinations serves to solve the problem of final grounding of determination in general: the determinations are fully concrete in that all of their moments are fully articulated. The logical determinations are thus absolute grounds of possibility of all determination (absolute in that they are not relative to whatever it is that is determined). Even the most contingent and empirical of sense data is determinate—and can enter consciousness—only to the extent that it is implicitly determined as some quality; and even the most strictly non-conceptual aspect of fact or of fiction, even if posited as wholly indeterminate and inaccessible to thought, is thereby posited precisely in and by thought, as inaccessible to it.

The ability of thought to determine the indeterminate as "indeterminate" suggests a further sense in which the Absolute Idea is "all truth": it is the "truest." The Absolute Idea is "truer" than any individual moment of the *Logic*, some moments of the *Logic* are "truer" than others, and some extralogical determinations and even things are "truer" than others. For Hegel, degrees of truth depend upon fullness of determinacy. Within the *Logic*, the categories are arranged atutomatically in order of increasing determinative adequacy; the arrangement is "automatic" in that the determination of any category, or of any thing in accordance with any category, is at the same time its determination in terms of all preceding categories. Thus, for example, "*x* is an entity" says very little about *x*, while "*x* is a thing," determining *x* as the sort of entity that remains self-identical despite the diversity and transitoriness of its properties, provides much more information. "X is a mechanical object"—that is, a thing within a mechanical system and thus obeying its laws—is a yet fuller determination. The categories increase in richness, in explicit content, and are thus, as applied, increasingly determinative. Correspondingly, the thing that may be *correctly* determined to be a mechanical object is "truer" than one that can be determined only as an entity.

The introduction of the notion of "correctness" brings up a final aspect of Hegel's doctrine of truth—and thus of the Absolute Idea as "all truth"—that must be briefly considered. Traditionally, "correctness" is taken to be determinable through formal logic alone, without reference to reality: a judgment is "correct" if it does not violate the laws of logic or grammar. This "correctness" is opposed to a "truth" that requires correspondence of the judgment to that to which it refers. In these terms, "The rose is red" and "The rose is black" are both *correct* in that in each a quality is predicated of an entity; "The rose is tiger" would be incorrect. In addition, "The rose is red" is *true* when appropriately used to describe a rose that is in fact red. This use of the terms is grounded in a notion of truth as correspondence, according to which a thought is true if it conforms to the thing of which it is the thought. Hegel refuses to grant to mere things such fundamental epistemological importance; consequently, he reverses the significations of truth and correctness. For Hegel, "The rose is red" does not deserve to be classed as "true," for it is, in isolation, incomplete: the rose is a flower and is alive, in addition to being red; there are other red things besides the rose; and the rose could equally well have been white or pink. "The rose is red" fails to determine, and thus to express the truth of, its subject, or its predicate, or its referent. One implication of this analysis is that no judgment, standing alone, can be true; rather, "the true is the whole (*PG*:21/PS:11)." At the same time, however, "The rose is red" may well be, in Hegelian terms, correct: it is if the rose is red. A second implication of Hegel's doctrine of truth is that contingencies cannot be true in the strict sense, even if they are actual, for they could be otherwise: only what must be as it is can be true rather than merely correct.[6] For this reason, the philosopher cannot be satisfied by the mere determination of matters of fact. Given "what is," the philosopher asks whether it is true (*TW*20:239); given "what happens," the philosopher seeks to determine which aspects of the actual process are true (*L*2:226/ *SL*:578). This teaching clearly has ramifications crucial to philosophy as science; they are considered below.

Hegel's claim with respect to the Absolute Idea should now be clear. It may be summarized as follows: first, only the Absolute Idea is fully determinate and thus fully true in and of itself, since in and of itself it explicitly contains all of the determinations of the *Logic*; second, the determinations of the *Logic* are themselves determinate, and thus true, only through their interrelationship in the Idea; third, extralogical determinations of thought are determinate only through relation to the grounded determinations of the *Logic*; and fourth, things are determinate only to the extent that they are subject to predication by determinations, all of which depend on the logical categories for their own functionality. The Absolute Idea is thus presented as a principle of determination satisfying the ontological demands of absoluteness, completeness, and correctness, and thereby grounding first philosophy.

Logic, Nature, Spirit

The Absolute Idea is an ontological rather than a theological principle. It is in no way established by the *Logic* as the real ground—the ground of being of what is; it is rather the ideal ground, the ground of determinacy, capable of determining itself and of grasping what is—should there be something, and should it somehow be given or accessible—through its own functional determinations. The Absolute Idea is not God, and the move to Nature is nothing like a creation, *ex nihilo* or otherwise. That transition and the sciences that follow must be interpreted, like the *Logic*, ontologically rather than cosmologically, psychologically, or theologically.

Schelling suggests one possible ontological interpretation for the move to the Philosophy of Nature. He acknowledges that the *Logic* might prove to the subject that it is infinite when it takes itself, or the realm of thought, as its object, but he stresses that the subject remains finite when it attempts to determine any real objectivity. To the extent that the logical subject is finite it will, according to Schelling, desire to explain itself and its world as fully as possible in terms of its logically derived categories. Only with the incorporation of factical existence into the system would the subject's internal diremption be overcome. This sort of transition would be neither theological nor cosmological, but it would violate Hegel's systematic demands in that it would be a move demanded by the finite rather than by the logical subject (its motivation would be extrasystematic), and would thus presuppose the factical world, as perceived by the individual subject, as a source of content for philosophy. If Hegel's transition were of this sort, then Schelling would be justified in complaining that the task becomes that of Hegel's reconstructing his own individual and contingent world view.

Not only would such a transition be in conflict with Hegel's principles, in addition, Hegel explicitly denies that the move to Nature is a move to the world as experienced (see *L*2:231/*SL*: 591-92). While the move cannot, if it is legitimate, be understood as a creation by or emanation from a supersensible entity, it also cannot be understood as an afterthought of the finite subject who realizes that the logical account is somehow incomplete. Rather, the move must be made by the subject qua absolute, the subject as Absolute Idea. The move is possible in that the *Logic*, while self-sufficient as the science of pure thought, points beyond itself toward a world made up of things. The notion of an extralogical reality is implicit in the *Logic* itself, for two reasons: (1) most of the categories would *apply* not to other categories—most are not applicable within the *Logic*—but rather to things that are not categories, and (2) the subject is Idea, rather than merely Concept, only in that its ability to determine a reality different from itself is, in principle, confirmed. This relation to the extralogical does not compromise the purity of the *Logic* or of the Idea. Neither any individual category nor the Absolute Idea is dependent for concreteness, determinacy, or reality—in the logical sense of distinctness from others—upon a factical realm. At the same time, the *Logic* shows that it makes sense to speak of a plur-

ality of existent things only if the things are understood as determined by a subject. This opens the way for further development.

As of the end of the *Logic*, the extralogical has not been thematized as such. Nevertheless, from the standpoint of the Absolute
Idea it is already clear that any extralogical realm would contain
finite entities and finite subjects concerned with their determination. The *Logic* itself includes categories that would be applicable
only within such a realm, but it does not include the specific categories that would make determination within the extralogical
realm posssible. The investigation of these additional categories is
a task different from that of the *Logic*, but not unrelated to it. The
philosopher on the level of the Idea already knows—from speculative rather than from sensory experience—that further categorial investigation of nature and spirit is possible. The philosopher
also knows that these investigations must develop the relevant
categories in the order of their increasing richness of determination; from the standpoint of the Idea, the method of the systematic sciences is known, as well as the general nature of their
contents. Since this is so, no extrasystematic impetus for the
transition from Logic to Nature need be postulated.

As categorial sciences, the Philosophies of Nature and Spirit
will directly consider neither our world nor us as human beings;
they will rather thematize, respectively, the categories fundamental to all possible worlds, and those essential to subjects confronted with worlds. If there is to be a real multiplicity, there must be
spatial extension, and if individual entities are to be individuals
(as multiplicity itself requires), they must exhibit continuity in
time; the first two categories in the Philosophy of Nature are, understandably, Space and Time. When the account of the categories essential to any world—any nature—as determinate is completed, the question of how finite subjects can use the categories in
sensory experience remains. The question arises when the finite
subject is thematized as such, as it must be in the first part of the
Philosophy of Spirit.

As studies of the general categories necessary for Nature and
Spirit, Hegel's systematic subsciences are the purely ontological
correlates to the special metaphysical disciplines of cosmology

and rational psychology. The degree to which Hegel's subsciences, as he presents them, are satisfactory need not be considered here. (The Philosophy of Spirit is considered below with the problem of the relation of theory to practice.) It should be noted that the Philosophy of Nature, which is often considered to be completely inadequate, is the part of the system on which Hegel worked the least. It is the shortest part of the *Encyclopedia*, and was never taught by Hegel in isolation. From the general realm of the Philosophy of Spirit, he published the *Philosophy of Right* as well as the *Phenomenology*, and he frequently gave special lecture courses on aspects of Spirit including Right, History, Aesthetics, Religion, and Philosophy. While it would therefore not be surprising if Hegel's Philosophy of Nature were less than perfect—as is clear from the *Logic*, speculative thought is a painstaking process that if not carefully practiced is likely to lose its purity—any legitimate criticism of it must apply to it as a categorial science. Such a science need not, for example, explain the universe in terms either of Newtonian or of Einsteinian physics. Whereas physics, and the empirical sciences in general, attempt to explain our universe, the categorial science must consider the conceptual conditions of possibility of any universe. From the categorial standpoint, either a unified field theory or a theory based in four distinct kinds of fundamental forces—or any of various other theories—might provide a "correct" description of the behavior of matter in our universe. Furthermore, a universe correctly describable in terms of a unified field theory would be "truer" than one that required four wholly distinct forces, since it would more closely correspond to the theoretical ideal of complete internal determination. Nevertheless, even that theory could never be "true" in the highest degree, since it could never be established that all possible realities would have to be structured in the same factual way.

RESPONSE TO SCHELLING

Successful response to Schelling's critique of the end of the *Logic* must, as is indicated above, be grounded in insistence that the

Absolute Idea is an ontological rather than a theological principle, and that the system based in it remains ontological throughout. Such insistence alone suffices to counter most of Schelling's
objections, for most are directed against the possibility of a transition from transcendental logic to transcendent theology. Ontologically interpreted, the transition to Nature does not rely on
identification of the Absolute Idea as God, and it does not signify
a real creation. Nor does the Philosophy of Nature purport to be a
reconstruction of the factical world as it is experienced by Hegel or
by anyone else. Finally, in this interpretation the relation of the
Absolute Idea to Absolute Spirit poses no fundamental problems.
At the end of the *Logic*, the subject knows itself as infinite in the
Absolute Idea; at the end of the system, it has reconfirmed that its
infinitude is retained even if it is confronted with a real nature. It
does not discover the truth of the latter by subjecting itself to a
real, temporal process whose reality is ultimately denied; since its
infinitude has already been logically established, its status is not
threatened by its consideration of Nature and Spirit.

While the ontological interpretation thus avoids the main
thrust of Schelling's attack, it must be acknowledged that Hegel's
prose is at least partly responsible for Schelling's reading. First,
Hegel's descriptions of the *Logic* as the determination of God or
the Absolute could encourage the reader to interpret the work
theologically. Nonetheless, the careful reader should recognize
that the intent of the work cannot be theological when, through
the failure of the Logic of Essence, it is revealed that even God
would not realize his absoluteness by creating a finite world to
which he would then be relative, by which he would then be limited. In that the Absolute Idea purports to be the complex principle of all determination, the categories of the *Logic* are presented
as the fundamental thoughts of God as well as of man; since this
is the case, the *Logic* is, metaphorically, the exhibition of the
thoughts of God "prior to the creation of nature and finite spirit."
The theological relevance of this teaching is presented in the Philosophy of Spirit, in the analysis of Religion, rather than in the
Logic; in the later account, the truth revealed in the *Logic* is reconfirmed when Religion is shown to give way to speculative philosophy.

A second locus of Hegelian terminological opacity is the account of the transition from Logic to Nature. It must be admitted that the descriptions there are obscure to the point of unintelligibility. That obscurity does not necessarily, however, indicate a systematic defect. While it would be difficult if not impossible to explain the transition adequately through direct interpretation of the page and a half of text Hegel devotes to it, it remains possible to explain it on the basis of an analysis of the Absolute Idea as principle and of the systematic structures that may be anticipated from the standpoint of the Idea; such an account is given above. It must further be stressed in this connection that there are various moves in the *Logic* which, like the move to Nature, involve steps from "subjective" to "objective" determinations (see esp. *E*:§193A), and although Hegel denies that the step to Nature is identical to any step within the *Logic*, one of the terms he uses to describe the move to Nature suggests that it can be compared to certain earlier developments. The term *entschliessen*, translated above as "deciding" or "resolving," and taken by Schelling to signify a subjective act of will, is used in the *Logic* to signify the relation of a Universal to the Particulars it contains implicitly, as moments that may be explicated (see *L*2:275/*SL*:636, *TW*17:408). In that, as has already been indicated, the "moments" of the Absolute Idea that could be further developed are visible, from the standpoint of the Idea, as falling within the spheres of Nature and Spirit, the "decision" to develop them characterizes a speculative-philosophical movement, and not a subjective whim.

A final Schellingian point must be considered. Schelling insists that whether the transition is taken ontologically or theologically, it signifies a break in the dialectical thread. Here, as often before, acknowledgement that Schelling's observation is accurate does not entail admission that he has discovered a systematic defect. There *is* a break in the dialectic in that the Philosophy of Nature does not begin with a further logical determination of the Absolute Idea itself; that would be impossible. Rather, the subject at the standpoint of the Absolute Idea sees the possibility of further dialectical development, he sees that the development would be structured in terms of Nature and Spirit, and he sees that the immediate move from the end of the *Logic* must be to the former rather than to the latter; his vision of these points is, again, made possible by the development of the *Logic* itself. There is no ungrounded contradiction forcing further dialectical development, but there is the possibility of speculative consideration of a new categorial realm. If that consideration is undertaken, it must begin with the positing of the aspect of its subject matter that presupposes no content or determination; the starting point for the subject matter "Nature" is Space. To the extent that the development that follows from the determination of Space is necessary rather than free, Hegel's fundamental contention that intelligibility is dialectically structured is supported. The "break" in the dialectic is then no indication of systematic incoherence.

The explanation of the transition from the *Logic* to the Philosophy of Nature completes the defense of Hegel's system. I have argued that if the *Logic* is interpreted ontologically, it remains true to its principles both as a self-grounding first philosophy and as a ground for categorial accounts of Nature and Spirit. Schelling's objections to Hegel's as a system of transcendental ontology have thus been overcome. Yet to be considered are his objections to ontology as such, the claims grounding his assertion that even if Hegel's system satisfies the Hegelian, it cannot satisfy the true philosopher.

PART TWO

The
Philosophical
Project

4

Metaphysics And Human Existence

Schelling's critique of the Hegelian system begins with the assertion that its fundamental thought, according to which "reason relates itself to the in-itself or essence of things" (13:60), is arbitrarily presupposed; the critique of the project develops from the claim that this thought, no matter how plausible it may be made to appear, remains a complete misconception. While the professional philosopher may find the notion of a science of essences intriguing, such a science cannot, Schelling insists, satisfy the legitimate philosophical demands of ordinary human beings faced with concrete existential problems. In Schelling's view, the domination of Hegel's system had for this reason led to a crisis for philosophy within a decade after its author's death:

> Never before has there arisen . . . so massive a reaction against philosophy as is visible at present. This proves that philosophy has come to the point of encounter with those questions of life in the face of which it is not permissible—indeed, not possible—for anyone to be indifferent. As long as philosophy is involved with its first beginnings or with the first stages of its development, it is the concern only of those who have made philosophy their lifework. All others await the end of philosophy; it becomes important for the world only in its results (14:363).

"The world" has waited for the results of philosophy, but those results—the teachings of Hegel—thwart the world's expectations: they seem to threaten life instead of supporting it, to destroy man's fundamental beliefs instead of grounding them. Man therefore cannot and will not, according to Schelling, accept Hegel's results. But there is the danger that the rejection of Hegel's system may be tantamount, in the view of common consciousness, to the rejection of philosophy itself; the verdict may be, "There shall be no more philosophy at all" (13:364).

Regardless of the internal consistency of Hegel's system and of the degree to which it satisfies Hegel's demands, Schelling insists that it fails if it does not satisfy the demands of ordinary human beings:

> Most study philosophy not in order to become philosophers, but rather to gain those great unifying convictions without which there is no intellectual self-sufficiency and no human dignity. Indeed, in a time when everything else has become questionable, when everything positive is beset with controversies and oppositions of all sorts, then it appears doubly important and necessary that a bold philosophy, one thoroughly acquainted with all the depths of spirit, rebuild and fortify the unsteady foundations of all true human conviction (9:359).

Schelling strongly encourages what he takes to be his students' expectations concerning his lectures. They should approach the lectures with the belief that:

> Here, I should get the answers to those questions for which no other science provides answers, those which, sooner or later, but unavoidably, trouble every honest spirit; here, the veil that has heretofore obscured not individual objects, but the *whole*, should be removed, revealing that whole of which I feel myself a part, but that seems to me to become the more inconceivable the more I know about individual things. Unquestionably, I should here gain those great convictions that maintain human consciousness, those without which life has no point, without which it would be devoid of all dignity and self-sufficiency (13:3, cf. *GPP*:68-69).

Schelling recognizes that the problems of the age may appear to be so great that nothing can be done, but insists:

> The more stridently the dissensions, the disputes, the phenomena that threaten dissolution, the more harshly these aspects of our time are presented, the more certainly will he who is truly informed see in all of them only the omens of a new creation, of a great and lasting revival; a revival that, admittedly, will not be possible without grievous misery, a creation that must be preceded by the ruthless destruction of all that has become lazy, fragile, and decayed. But there must be an end to this struggle because, despite the common belief to the contrary, there can be no endless, no pointless and senseless progress. It is therefore to be anticipated that the striving for wisdom will also reach its long-sought goal, where the unrest that has plagued the human spirit for many thousands of years will cease, where man will finally come to master the real organism of his information and his knowledge; where, over all the parts of human knowledge that have before been separate and mutually exclusive, there will flow the spirit of universal mediation, like a balm that heals all the wounds that human spirit has inflicted upon itself in its zealous struggle for light and truth, wounds from which our time still bleeds (13:10-11).

Schelling further recognizes that many will doubt that it is philosophy that can heal the ills of the age, and acknowledges that the history of philosophy may seem to justify such doubt. He stresses, however, that it is a mistake to take Hegelianism as a philosophical paradigm:

> ... when I see in philosophy the means of healing the dismemberment that characterizes our time, I of course do not mean a weak philosophy, a mere artifact, I mean a strong philosophy, one that can measure itself by life, one that, far from feeling powerless in the face of life and its atrocious realities, far from being limited to the sorry occupation of mere negation and destruction, would take its force from reality itself and would then also produce something actual and lasting (13:11).

Schelling thus promises a new teaching, one that will "measure itself by life" rather than by the abstract criteria of the professional philosopher; but he realizes that the promise may sound empty, he knows from his own experience that none of the nearly countless philosophical doctrines that man has produced has answered the crucial questions, and he knows that, in the face of the impotence of reason that seems thereby to be revealed, resignation is tempting (13:14). Yet, he continues, there has been, quite recently, real and obvious progress in the empirical sciences, which have focused on the existent world; there have been scientific discoveries "through which human spirit has been liberated, broadened, and really placed on a higher level." It may be, Schelling suggests, that philosophy should learn from this example:

> The world does not care whether some Roman author wrote *declarabat* or *declamabat;* the question of whether the deduction of categories should begin with the category of quantity, as it has, with good reason, from the time of Aristotle up until quite recently, or with that of quality, as has been popularized by a more recent logic, perhaps only because it did not know quite how to start with quantity—that is perhaps not entirely unimportant to scholars, but in the world, nothing is thereby changed in the least (13:27).

Schelling is eager to agree with "the world" that such abstruse philological and logical considerations cannot answer the questions posed by life itself, but he denies both that the scholarly concerns are the most truly philosophical ones and that the answers to the existential questions can be found by any discipline other than philosophy. The truly philosophical is of necessity the metaphysical: "True metaphysics is honor, it is virtue, true metaphysics is not only religion, it is also respect for the law and love of the fatherland." The "end and result" of a philosophy satisfied with the logical description of categories could be nothing other than the moral doctrine derived by Shakespeare's Falstaff, in far simpler fashion, in the catechism that teaches that since honor is a mere word, and words nothing but air, "honor is a mere scutcheon (13:27)."

As Schelling's reference to Falstaff indicates, the most important ill of the age is nihilism, the doctrine that there are no absolute values, that matters of right and wrong are thus matters of opinion. The common man can recognize the failure of Hegel's system in its inability to overcome nihilism. Schelling, a philosopher, is concerned also with revealing why Hegel's system, as a doctrine merely of essences, cannot possibly pass this crucial test. By restricting himself to essences, Schelling asserts, Hegel dooms himself to the sort of one-sided treatment in which a mere moment is taken to be the whole truth; such one-sidedness is the source of "all errors and hindrances of true insight into science" (14:249). Hegel's system can appear to be all-encompassing, Schelling insists, only because it is in fact limited to an easily manipulable subject matter:

> Nothing is more conceivable than the concept, and he who takes it as the object of his development has chosen the most compliant material. The actual concept is only an act of thought. The inconceivable first starts with what is *opposed* to the concept....Nothing is easier than transportation into pure thought, but it is not so easy to come back out of it again. The world does not consist of mere categories or pure concepts, it does not consist of concrete *concepts*, but rather of concrete and contingent things, and the matter at hand is the illogical, the other, which is *not* the concept but its opposite, which only unwillingly accepts the concept. It is here that philosophy is put to the test (*GPP*:225).

In that it remains throughout within the realm of thought, "Hegel's entire philosophy is nothing other than an Eleaticism, revitalized with the help of its method and thus given the semblance of new life" (*GPP*:218). Hegel may have succeeded in articulating the One that lies at the end of the Parmenidean Way of Truth, but he has not brought it into relation with the Way of Opinion constitutive of the world in which we actually live: "We live in this determinate world, not in an abstract or universal world that we so much enjoy deluding ourselves with by holding fast only to the most *universal* properties of things, without penetrating into their actual relationships" (14:332). Hegel accounts for:

> ...the mere negative of existence, that *without* which nothing can exist; but from this it by no means follows that everything exists only

through it. It can be the case that everything is within the logical Idea, without it thereby being the case that anything is thus *explained*, as for example everything in the sensible world is included in number and measure, without it thereby being the case that geometry or arithmetic explains the sensible world (10:143; cf. 11:284-85, *GPP*:222-23).

For Schelling, then, Hegel—like Fichte—is unable to derive or account for a true objectivity:

> We can produce everything that comes forth in our experience in pure thought, but then it is *only* in thought. If we wanted to transform this into an objective claim—to say that everything is, in itself, merely in thought—then we would have to return to the standpoint of a Fichtean idealism.

Schelling's Fichte, it will be recalled, fails to derive a true objectivity because he begins his account with the individual human ego. Since that ego is not conscious of being the creator of the world, it cannot generate the world from itself; its speculations, like Hegel's logical ones, are arbitrary fantasies rather than necessary constructions. Fichte fails because he does not realize that the being that is the source of objectivity—that "through which" everything exists—must be the source of subjectivity as well, and must therefore be prior to thought as well as to things:

> . . . if we want [to derive or account for] any being that is outside of thought, then we must start from a being that is absolutely independent of all thinking, that precedes all thinking. Of this being, the Hegelian philosophy knows nothing; for this concept, it has no place (13:164).

Differently stated: Hegel's system has no place for the transcendent being—the supersensible source of being—precisely because that being cannot be conceptualized. As Schelling takes Kant to have proved, the highest being cannot be grasped by a philosophy having access only to moments of thought, because the thought of God is the thought of "the being that is before all thinking" (13:163).

According to Schelling, then, because Hegel's system does not begin with God, it can never reach the world or man; if philosophy is to account for sensible entities, it must first account for the supersensible entity that grounds them. The truly comprehensive system must begin with the highest being, and must end with finite beings. Its dialectic can lead from the one to the other, according to Schelling, only if it results from the transformation of real principles, not merely of thoughts (11:331-32). The true science of pure thought is an objective idealism, one that considers "actual ideas (ideas of things), not abstract concepts" (11:465-66).

These objections begin to indicate just how fundamental Schelling's first-philosophical opposition to Hegel really is. The opposition is as first obscured by the agreement of the two that first philosophy must be the "free science, produced by thought alone," and that it must begin with the *primum cogitabile*, the "first thinkable." The agreement is superficial. For Hegel, the *primum cogitabile* is the thought that is logically first, that is, the concept that presupposes no prior determination. For Schelling, the *primum cogitabile* that alone can ground philosophy is the entity that can be thought without contradiction as absolutely prior, the entity capable of grounding its own existence and of functioning as the source of all other beings. For Hegel, first philosophy is transcendental ontology, the science of the determinations fundamental to things and to thought; for Schelling, it must be transcendent theology, the science of the highest being.

The opposition of Hegel and Schelling with respect to philosophy's starting point entails an equally fundamental opposition with respect to dialectic, the way in which thought produces its "free science." As is indicated above, Schelling insists that the truly objective dialectic must be a movement of principles, not one merely of thoughts. The rejection of categories in favor of principles is seen by Schelling as at least suggested by both Plato and Aristotle. With respect to the former, Schelling asserts that "the core of Platonic wisdom is [in the *Philebus*]; but it is preceded by the *Sophist*, the true inaugural hymn of higher science" (11:393). In Schelling's view, what is traditionally known as Plato's doctrine of ideas—according to which the ideas are eternal models or paradigms of things—is brought to its peak with the Eleatic Stranger's account of a *symploke* of highest genera; what becomes visible from that peak, however, is that philosophy is truly concerned with the intellectual intuition of subjects—of self-sufficient moving principles—rather than of predicates. Plato's highest teaching is given in the *Philebus*, in the Socratic account of the Pythagorean principles, an account Schelling claims to complete with his own dialectic of subjective and objective powers.

With respect to the nature of the ideas, according to Schelling, Plato's insight was deeper than Aristotle's. The latter's investigation of the highest principles begins with his assertion that what is intellectually intuited—as the first principles must be—can only be the nonsynthetic (*asyntheta*), and so cannot be composed of potency and act, or of subject and predicate. There are two sorts of "simples" (*hapla*) that come into question. There are those that are purely active, the pure subjects such as God or, somewhat less clearly, the stars (11:352), but pure predicates or potencies are also simples. Schelling criticizes Aristotle for not emphasizing with sufficient clarity that the predicates are at best means to the subjects, that *archai* are far more philosophically important than *kategoriai* (11:353,303). Schelling himself insists on the point, going so far as to exclude the latter, despite their "simplicity," from the realm of apodictic evidential givenness:

> The *symploke* of potency and act is what is potentially deceptive (*der Täuschung zugängliche*). But with respect to the purely active (*reine energeia*), no deception is possible. The predicates are however mere potencies (11:325n).

In opposition to Hegel, Schelling insists that first philosophy must be theology, and that its dialectic must be real. Hegel has of course denied—in the *Logic*, the *Phenomenology*, and the Philosophy of Spirit—not only that special metaphysics is possible, but also that it is desirable. According to Hegel, when reason comprehends the true nature of theology, both as religion and as the philosophical attempt to ground the world metaphysically in a transcendent entity, it comprehends at the same time that and why reason must seek—and can attain—satisfaction elsewhere. Schelling counters first with the assertion that Hegel's claim is effective at best only against the kinds of theological doctrines that he has been able to imagine: "what if, some day, wholly new concepts of philosophy were to be found?" (GPP:222). He makes the objection sharper by asserting that such a "new concept" of philosophy has already appeared:

> Fifty years ago, Kant believed himself to have traversed and exhausted the entire realm of human faculties of knowledge; later, the attempt was made to circumscribe the entire realm of the concept and all possible conceptual moments within a logical circle. Closer observation reveals however that only those concepts were included that were given in the contingent world view of the time. Already in the present development, many [new] concepts and conceptual movements have come to the fore, ones of which those attempts had no inkling. Those attempts related themselves to the world as their agents found it before them, the world they knew; in these lectures, a new world has revealed itself to us, one of which they knew simply nothing, which they could in no way take up in the circles of their concepts except through complete distortion. This may serve as warning against premature terminations of philosophy and the swaggering that accompanies them. The fact of a Philosophy of Revelation shows already that there was still an entire world left over that was not embraced by previous philosophies (14:292-93).

It is, then, Schelling's own final system that proves Hegel's vision limited: "Positive philosophy is a new discovery that is especially inopportune [for those] who maintain that philosophy had already been completed" (13:120).

Schelling's positive philosophy purports to overcome both the technical defects of Hegelianism—defects visible and thus of immediate importance only to the professional philosopher—and the great existential problem of the age, the despair that often accompanies the conviction that, since nothing has any absolute worth, life is meaningless and human activity devoid of significance. The practical problem can be overcome, Schelling insists, only through the theologically grounded conviction that the process in which man is caught up is, on the whole, wisely ordered:

> Man finds himself, from the beginning of his existence, thrown into a stream whose movement is independent of him, a stream that he cannot immediately resist and that he must therefore, at first, suffer; yet he is not meant to allow himself to be simply pushed around by this stream like a dead object, he should learn to grasp the meaning of the movement in order to be able to further it, instead of vainly attempting to resist, and also in order to be able to precisely distinguish what, independent of himself, happens in accord with and in opposition to this meaning, not in order always directly to confront the latter, but in order to redirect the evil, so far as is possible, to the good, and to use the power or energy developed by what should not be to further the true movement. Assuming however that man had convinced himself, through the most careful investigation possible, that this movement was completely blind from the beginning, and therefore either had no end—that it would proceed infinitely and pointlessly (so that history would have no goal)—or that it had an end that would be reached blindly, resulting from a blind necessity; if man had become convinced of this, then if he did not embrace something like the stoic's unnatural struggle against an indomitable fate, [1] he would probably decide to subordinate himself to this inexorable and unavoidable movement and to exclude it as much as possible from his own activities; but this decision would clearly be a clever rather than a wise one. If man is to order his life wisely, that is, with wisdom, he must presuppose that there is wisdom in the movement itself. For only then can he give himself to it of his own free will, that is, as a wise man (13:202-203).

Schelling's use of "wisdom" in this passage clarifies his conception of philosophy as the love of wisdom. On the existential level, wisdom is essentially practical: to be wise is to "order one's life wisely." According to Schelling, this practical wisdom has two presuppositions. First, human beings must be existentially free: if they were merely "dead objects," they would be unable to order their own lives, they would be "simply pushed around" in the stream of being. The second presupposition of true practical wisdom is that there is "wisdom in the movement itself." If good acts cannot be distinguished from evil and indifferent ones, if a life devoted to the satisfaction of individual and contingent desires is as defensible as any other, then human beings may exhibit cleverness—they may show themselves apt in discovering convenient means to those arbitrary and temporary ends—but they will never exhibit wisdom.

The grounds for Schelling's objections to Hegel's conception of the philosophical endeavor should now be generally clear; yet, as Schelling himself acknowledges, those objections are forceful only if there is a viable theological alternative to Hegel's program. Evaluation of the objections therefore presupposes determination of the viability of Schelling's own metaphysical program. Schelling insists that his positive philosophy is a novel theology, one wholly unforeseen by Hegel. He insists in addition that positive philosophy, and only positive philosophy, can overcome the threat of nihilism. It is therefore to Schelling's final system, the tradition's final metaphysical theology, that we now must turn.

5

Schellingian Positive Philosophy

PREHISTORY: THE SYSTEM OF IDENTITY

While Schelling insists that his final system—which he calls positive philosophy—overcomes the limitations of Hegelianism, he denies that that system originated as a reaction to Hegel's. As is indicated above (pp. 49–50), Schelling was predisposed by his own reflections to see in Hegel's *Logic* an attempt at further progress along a path that he already knew to be a philosophical dead end. In 1802, in the dialog *Bruno*, Schelling dramatizes the conflict between the true metaphysician—who seeks the real ground of what is—and the mere ontologist, who seeks to ground knowledge while denying human access to the ground of being. The merely ontological position is represented by the character Lucian, an avatar of Fichte. Lucian argues that consciousness would have to transcend itself in order to reach its own ground, and that such transcendence is in principle impossible. He concludes that "we have no ground, in philosophizing, for going beyond the pure consciousness that is given in grounded consciousness, or for considering the former in any way save in relation to the latter, whose principle it is" (4:253).[1] We can thus, according to Lucian, examine only human consciousness, a consciousness that is not responsible for its own existence—or that, at least, can never be directly aware of itself as grounding its existence. We can grasp at most how and why we think of things as we do; we cannot know either how things really are, or why they are as they are (4:256).

Lucian does not deny that the philosopher can posit a transcendent absolute, but he insists that there can be no move from the thought of the absolute to grounded certainty of the existence of a being correspondent to the thought. Bruno, a transcendent metaphysician, agrees with Lucian only in part. He acknowledges that no discussion of the absolute in abstraction from what it grounds could possibly prove that the absolute exists. He takes upon himself, as theologian, a stronger burden of proof. He can establish that the absolute ground he posits is in fact the ground of what is only by showing "how the emergence—with which consciousness is connected—out of the eternal is to be grasped not merely as possible, but as necessary," explaining "the descent of the finite from the eternal . . . from the standpoint of the eternal itself, without presupposing anything other than the highest idea" (4:257).

In the dialog, Bruno gives such an account of the "descent of the finite from the eternal," and Lucian finds the account completely convincing. Bruno then leads Lucian to admit that even a system satisfying the more modest demands he had earlier articulated would fail to satisfy the demands of philosophy:

> BRUNO: Is it not true that a philosophy grounded in such a knowledge will completely exhibit the contents (*Inbegriff*) of common consciousness, and be totally in accord with it, without—for just that reason—being philosophy at all?
> LUCIAN: Without a doubt (4:327).

The conflict in the dialog foreshadows the conflict between Schelling and Hegel. Schelling is convinced in advance that the *Logic*, if merely ontological, can—at least in principle—accurately "exhibit the contents of common consciousness," but that it will not thereby complete philosophy. At the same time, he requires for the successful overcoming of Hegel the presentation of a compelling and comprehensive theological system that will explain the descent of the finite from the infinite.

The basic strategy of Schelling's dialectic is described above (pp. 16, 46–48). In the *Exhibition of My System of Philosophy* (1801), Schelling schematizes the method in a manner that he retains throughout the rest of his career. The development of content begins with the primal self-reflection in which two moments come to be distinguished within the identity of the absolute. Since the absolute is absolute, however, it remains self-identical even in its self-reflection. The first dialectical moment is therefore presented as the identity $A = B$. The unity of the absolute is thus retained, but since A is subjective (the absolute reflecting on itself) and B objective (the absolute objectified by itself), the moment is one of merely "relative identity." A and B do not differ in terms of content—A knows only B, and B is as it is known by A—but since the one knows while the other is known, the moment is, as one of merely relative identity, necessarily one of "relative difference." B has been posited by A, but A remains unposited. The moment becomes one of "relative totality" only when it is posited as a whole, as $A = B$. The absolute now qua positor of $A = B$ is designated A^2. The complex then present is $A^2 = (A = B)$ (see §57A), but that is a new moment of relative identity, and as such requires a higher subjective power if it is to be made into a totality.

At every moment in Schelling's process, identity is claimed to be retained in that every objective moment that arises is known—or posited—by a subjective moment that fully corresponds to it in terms of content and complexity. If, for example, $A = B$ is compared to $A^2 = (A = B)$, the two may appear to be essentially different, but the comparison is the work only of "arbitrary reflection." Philosophical speculation is concerned not with such merely apparent differences but with the whole, the entire range of developing identities of various powers of subjectivity and objectivity. Where the arbitrarily reflecting subject will see the plant as relatively defective in "knowing" less than the animal, and the world of the animal as less complete than that of the human, the philosopher will see instead that the world grasped by the plant is in perfect harmony with the plant's needs and capacities, and that the same is true for all subjects.

While all subjects thus correspond to their objects, in most cases the unity is not absolute because the subject does not objectify itself; the identity remains relative. The process of generation of increasingly articulated identities must therefore continue until there arises a subject that is fully self-reflexive, one that grasps itself along with its object. This would be the "form of absolute self-knowledge" (§50E1).

Schelling's dialectic begins concretely when the first objective power, prime matter, is "posited" by primal light. The entire system would include the development of this minimal $A = B$ to the point of the emergence of the organism where, as the subjective comes to be preponderant over the objective, the philosophy of nature would give way to the philosophy of spirit. The latter would follow human spirit from its origin to its culmination, to the point where the absolute knows itself through man as fully as the human perspecive allows, or where man achieves an adequate self-reflection. In the published works in which Schelling's aim is purely scientific—as opposed to rhetorical or pedagogical[2] —the system is not covered in its entirety. In the *Exhibition*, the stage of the organism is reached, and in the *Further Exhibitions from the System of Philosophy* (1802), which might be expected to take up where the previous work leaves off, Schelling instead devotes much space once again to the beginning of the movement, and in the constructions that follow he provides additional detail on inorganic nature, especially on the organization of the solar system, but he does not even reach the level of the organism.

Although Schelling never published a complete construction of nature, much less of spirit, he seems to have been well pleased with the details of "dynamic physics" that he does cover. He sees in his general view of nature the correction of one of the fundamental errors of modernity, the theory, put forth most influentially by Descartes, that nature is static and thus subject only to and fully explicable by mechanical laws (see 7:15n). He stresses that this is among the most serious of Fichte's misconceptions (4:359, 7:7-9, 7:17). Schelling takes the mechanical view to be erroneous in itself, and to be a great hindrance to scientific progress insofar as it encourages merely empirical theorizing:

Whenever empirical science attempts to express something universal, it can always expect only to be refuted by later experience, whereas the theory that is derived, mediately or immediately, and more or less consciously, from the ideas or from construction can always be only confirmed by experience (4:473).

The superiority of his mode of theorizing is revealed, Schelling continues, by his prediction of the existence of the "planet" Pallas (now classed an asteroid), whose discovery shocked empirical astronomers:

It is well known to those with whom I have communicated my ideas over the years or who have attended my lectures that I maintained, on grounds taken from my doctrine of cohesion in the system of planets, not only the existence of a planet between Mars and Jupiter, but even characterized this position as the point of greatest density in the system of planets (4:473).

The discovery of Pallas is seen by Schelling as a dramatic confirmation of his most complete construction, that of the solar system, the account of which concludes:

If the simple and unforced agreement of all appearances in general can serve as test of a principle and of the theory grounded in it, then it must at least be granted that our principle—which of course derives its confirmation from higher grounds—does not fail to pass. There are admittedly a few determinations still lacking from the circle sketched here: but they also will enter in the future, e.g. the determinations of the distances of the planets from each other and from the center (4:507).

The only criticism of his natural constructions that Schelling seems seriously concerned to counter is that claiming that he can construct only those phenomena already discovered empirically. His prediction of the existence of Pallas is presented as one counterexample and, later, in response to Fichte's insistence that Schelling's theory could be confirmed only by successful predictions concerning otherwise unknown phenomena, Schelling defends himself by asserting that, at a time when magnetism was for empirical physicists no more than "the property of a single metal," he had already presented it as the "necessary category of matter" that later experiments clearly confirmed it to be (7:108).

The question of whether Schelling's satisfaction with his philosophy of nature is justified need not be considered here for, although he clearly spent a great deal of his time on his constructions of inorganic nature, his own demands are such that regardless of their adequacy in themselves, such constructions cannot alone confirm his principles or complete his system. The actual —as opposed to merely posited—efficacy of his absolute is confirmable only through correspondence of his constructions to the factical world as experienced, and whereas increasing fullness of detail with respect to inorganic nature could lend increasing credibility to the undertaking, the project embraced by Bruno—and presented as crucial to the positive refutation of Lucian/Fichte— requires the construction of consciousness, and thus an account of the human subject (4:257,282).

Schelling first attempts to account for the individual subject in the *System of Transcendental Idealism* of 1800; in an overview of the development of the *System*, he indicates how the subject will enter:

> Anyone can consider himself to be the object of these investigations. In order however to explain himself, he must first overcome all individuality in himself, because that is what is to be explained. If all the limitations of individuality are taken away, nothing remains save absolute intelligence. If the limits of intelligence are then overcome, nothing remains save the absolute ego. The problem then is this: how to explain absolute intelligence through an act of the absolute ego, and then how to explain, from an act of absolute intelligence, the entire system of limitedness that constitutes my individuality (3:483).

The final step here described by Schelling involves a fundamental difficulty: what necessity is there that, in moving from the transindividual to the individual level, I reconstruct the "system of limitedness that constitutes *my* individuality" rather than that constitutive of someone else? The problem, invisible to Schelling, arises for Proust as that of how the individual, after losing himself entirely in deep sleep, manages always to find himself again upon waking:

> How then, seeking for one's mind, one's personality, as one seeks for a thing that is lost, does one recover one's own self rather than any other? Why, when one begins again to think, is it not another personality that is incarnate in one? One fails to see what can dictate the choice, or why, among the millions of human beings any one of whom one might be, it is on him who one was overnight that unerringly one lays one's hand?[3]

For the sleeper as for the Schellingian philosopher, the reacquisition of a unique personality is possible only if the individual has never ceased to be himself, and only if his individuality can be determinative even when there is no consciousness of it. The constant presence and influence of what is unique in the subject, for Proust a fascinating phenomenon, is for Schelling one that must be denied: if individuality is determinative in this fashion, then the reconstructive process as a whole remains relative to the individual, and so can make no claim to absolute validity. If I can reconstruct only my personality, then I can never reflectively transcend my personal world; if philosophical construction is to be universally valid, it must finally either include all individuals, or stop short of the level of individuality.

The latter way of avoiding the problem is adopted by Schelling in the 1801 *Exhibition*. There Schelling insists that the philosopher must view all from the speculative standpoint, that the viewpoint of the individual is that of "arbitrary reflection." As has been indicated, however, neither the *Exhibition* nor the *Further Exhibitions* reveals how the human realm is to be included in the system. There is only one scientifically structured work that does cover the system in its entirety: the *System of All Philosophy and of the Philosophy of Nature in Particular*, a work completed in 1804 but published only posthumously. Since Schelling was by no means hesitant to publish in his early years, it should perhaps be suspected that he was not satisfied with his comprehensive presentation of the system; and indeed, with respect to the subject, the 1804 *System* does reveal problems that cannot be solved within the framework of the system of identity, problems that lead to the development of positive philosophy.

In the 1804 *System*, Schelling begins his treatment of the subject by insisting upon the fundamental continuity of humanity with other finite entities: he explicitly denies any capacity of existential freedom that would negate full dependence upon—and determination by—the natural order. This teaching represents a complete reversal on Schelling's part. In his earliest writings, he insists that while practical philosophy *presupposes* that human beings freely determine their own acts, even the "lowest degree of spontaneity" revealed in theoretical philosophy—the capacity of the subject to focus its attention as it chooses, a capacity without which there could be no consciousness of objects—*reveals* the subject's primordial freedom (1:205). For the Schelling of 1794, indeed, "the beginning and end of all philosophy is freedom" (1:177).

While Schelling's reversal with respect to the problem of human freedom is at first shocking, it is by no means evidence of simple inconsistency; it is, rather, entailed by the principles of the system of identity. The dialectical reconstruction constitutive of that system is possible only if the primal self-reflective act—which the philosopher can, at least in principle, imitate—completely determines all aspects of the factical world. Since the acts of human beings, like all other finite occurrences, follow in one way or another from the primordial act of the absolute, "The individual acts of will in the soul are always necessarily determined, and therefore not free, not absolute" (6:538). The notion of existential freedom and the problems, such as that of the origin of evil, that arise with it, result from the same sort of arbitrary reflection "that has borne into science all errors, all one-sided and false systems" (6:541). This sort of reflection leads to the comparison of individuals to each other, and thereby to the impression that some are "better" than others—an impression as mistaken as the belief that plants are inferior to animals (see p. 107, above). It is avoided by the philosopher, who views the whole rather than isolated parts: ". . . as necessarily as it belongs to the essence of the square not to be round, just so necessarily does it belong. . . to the essence of the blind person that he does not see; for if his seeing were compatible with the order of nature, then he would actually see" (6:543). Similarly,

> the desire and intention of harming others is considered, in man, to be evil, or something evil. But considered in itself, and if we look only to what is positive in the act, to the activity visible therein and so forth, in a word, if we consider the act absolutely, not in its relation to the subject, that is, comparing the latter with a universal concept, or with other men, then we will perceive therein a sort of completeness, in no way an incompleteness. Even the fact that this activity is expressed only in that which harms others is, considered in itself, no privation, for it belongs to the nature of this man just as necessarily as its opposite does not (6:544).

It might at first appear that Schelling's affirmation of complete metaphysical determinism, although opposed to his earlier teaching, is fully consistent in the context of the system of identity. The matter is, however, not so simple: the problem of freedom is intimately related to that of the descent of the finite from the infinite. As early as 1795, Schelling's writings reveal his conviction that this problem is the true source of all philosophical conflict (1:294). At that time, he also insists that the absolute itself can never become finite, and that there can be no distinct finite realm, for such would contradict the absoluteness of the absolute (1:288,308). It is a central tenet of the system of identity that the unity of the absolute is never destroyed, but at the same time, if human consciousness is to be explained, the origin of the illusion that there are finite, mutually exclusive entities must be accounted for. The extent of Schelling's perplexity concerning this problem—whose solution is "the main business of all philosophy (1:369)—is suggested by the fact that, in the 1804 *System*, he attempts to solve it in three inconsistent ways.

According to the 1804 *System*—and to the *Exhibition*—the absolute's primal self-reflection gives rise to "ideas," but the ideas are unified in the infinitude of the absolute. From this it is said to follow that

> ...from the standpoint of reason there is no finitude at all, that, therefore, no question can be raised concerning the origin of this finitude from God, for only the infinite emanates from God; that, moreover, to consider things as finite is not to consider them as they are in themselves (6:161).

While there can be no direct emanation of the finite from the absolute, the finite can emerge from God, according to one of Schelling's arguments, in an indirect or mediate fashion. The argument, present only in the 1804 *System*, is that the positing of the ideas as united in the absolute is also the non-positing of them as separate, that the positing of them as *being* only *in themselves*—as united in the absolute—is necessarily the positing of them as *not* being *for themselves*—as mutually distinct. Relative to the absolute the ideas qua separate from each other are nothing, but, Schelling insists strongly if nearly unintelligibly:

> A relative non-being includes, as such, a relative being within itself. That which relative to something—here, the absolute—is *absolutely* not, cannot, *not* so related, be absolutely not, for otherwise it would have to be, in the relation, absolutely (6:190).

Neither the precise meaning nor the potential adequacy of this obscure doctrine need be considered here;[4] for present purposes, it is important only to note that this teaching presents the absolute itself as responsible—albeit indirectly—for the existence of the finite.

Much later in the *System*, Schelling introduces a second explanation of the origin of the finite. After having denied all human freedom, Schelling proceeds, almost immediately, with what appears to be a retraction. The finitude of beings as individual, earlier asserted to be an indirect result of the absolute's primal thesis, and to be necessary to the revelation of the fullness of the divine infinite, is now said to result from a fall or defection of the finite from the absolute; it results from the ideas' primal sin of taking themselves, in mutual isolation, to be the highest reality (6:552). How this defection is possible is not explained, but the fall is clearly understood as volitional and thus presupposes a sort of freedom at least prior to the fall. The new doctrine, which would at least make an opening for a treatment of real freedom, may be more than merely an attempt to improve upon the obscure "indirect position" explanation of finitude. If his own activity as a philosopher is not to be senseless, then Schelling must somehow allow for human freedom. The presentation of philosophical argument—or any other kind of argument—makes sense only on the presupposition that those who encounter the argument may be convinced by it, not that there be a predetermined necessity that they change their minds, but that they be led to do so by the cogency of the argumentation. Schelling himself intends to convince those who believe themselves to need a moral god—and especially those who might otherwise be convinced by such doctrines—that his is the true teaching. He must thus assume in his audience a sort of freedom that his system often seems to deny. The fall doctrine could ground a presentation of human beings as free, but it is not so used in the *System*, and Schelling continues, having introduced it, to insist upon full determination within the human realm.

Having first made the absolute indirectly responsible for the origin of the finite, and then suggested that the finite is the source of its own existence qua separate from the absolute, Schelling offers, near the end of the *System*, a third creation doctrine, one making the absolute directly responsible: "This is the greatest secret of the universe, that the finite as finite can and should become like the infinite; God gives the ideas of the things that are in him over into finitude so that they can, through eternal reconciliation, be eternally in him as self-sufficient, as having life in themselves" (6:575). This doctrine does not present finite beings as coming to be through their own free acts, but it does entail the affirmation of existential freedom: the moral "can and should" is applicable to the finite entities only if they are free, only if they are capable of choosing to act either as they should or otherwise.

The presence in the 1804 *System* of three inconsistent creation doctrines, and the contradiction between the explicit denial and implicit entailment of existential freedom, many have been sufficiently clear to Schelling to keep him from publishing the work. In fact, he never presents a scientifically structured work in which both the problems of creation and those of human freedom are treated consistently. For the development of his reflections on these difficulties, three works which are pedagogically rather than scientifically structured must be considered: *Bruno*, "Philosophy and Religion" (1804), and *Philosophical Investigations Concerning the Essence of Human Freedom and Related Subjects* (1809).

In *Bruno*, as in one of the 1804 *System's* teachings, the finite is presented as responsible for its own separate existence:

> . . . everything that seems to emerge or free itself from [the absolute] unity is, in it, determined with respect to its possibility of being for itself, but the actuality of its separate existence lies only in itself, and takes place merely ideally, and as ideal only to the extent that a thing, in accord with its mode of being in the absolute, is made capable of being, in itself, unity (4:282).

While this account does have the advantage of providing the basis for a doctrine of human freedom, it wins that advantage only by introducing an element of indeterminacy into the world process. It thereby endangers the enterprise of Schellingian philosophical construction. If there is a multiplicity of ideas, each of which may or may not "turn away" from the absolute and thereby enter into a finite temporal process, then it would seem to be impossible to construct *a priori* the movement from infinite to finite, or the movement within the finite realm itself.

The threat to the constructive project is not recognized in *Bruno*, and in the dialog's sequel, "Philosophy and Religion," a similar creation doctrine is presented. There, however, a significant development is visible. If the absolute is ever to come to know itself through its self-objectifications, then its products, the ideas, must possess the fundamental characteristic of the absolute itself: they must be capable of autonomously attempting to objectify themselves. "The absolute would not be truly objective in [the ideas] if it did not communicate to [them] the power of transforming [their own] ideality into reality and objectifying [themselves] in particular forms" (6:135). The ideas must be free:

The peculiarity exclusive to the absolute is that it endows its antithesis [(the ideas)] with its own self-sufficiency along with its own essence. This being-in-itself, this authentic and true reality of that which is first intuited by the absolute, is *freedom*, and from that first self-sufficiency of the antithesis flows forth that which appears again in the world of appearance as freedom, there as the last trace and at the same time the seal of the divinity visible in the fallen world. The antithesis, as an absolute that has all properties in common with the first, would not be truly absolute and in itself were it not able to grasp itself in its selfhood, in order truly to be the *other* absolute. But it cannot be as the *other* absolute without thereby separating itself from the true absolute, or falling from it (6:39-40).

The doctrine of the fall is now presented as central to Schelling's thought: "The significance of a philosophy that makes the principle of the sinful fall, expressed in its highest universality, its own principle...cannot be overvalued" (6:43). Schelling does not seem to realize that this principle can scarcely ground his system of identity; he does not acknowledge that it makes the *a priori* reconstruction of the finite realm, at least in its historical totality, impossible; he does not note that entities that are free are knowable only through what they do. His principle cannot establish a science, there can be no account of the ideas in their infinite ineffability, and events resulting from free actions cannot be constructed *a priori*.

Early in the essay *Philosophical Investigations Concerning the Essence of Human Freedom*—the last major work published by Schelling himself—it becomes clear that Schelling is aware of the problem implicit in his system of identity. He asserts that his systematic writings have overcome the traditional opposition between nature and spirit, clearing the way for consideration of the truly fundamental philosophical problem: "It is time that the higher or, better, the authentic opposition step forth, that of necessity and freedom, with which the innermost central point of philosophy first comes into view" (7:333). In this essay, Schelling explicitly acknowledges that free beings can be known only through what they do, and takes the fully consequent step to the assertion that the absolute, as free, is also knowable only through what it does, that is, through the world it has created. This step makes the system of identity, as the *a priori* construction of what must follow from the primal thesis, impossible; but it also opens the way for the metaphysical empiricism of Schellingian positive philosophy.

METAPHYSICAL EMPIRICISM

It is a central contention of Kant's *Critique of Pure Reason* that only a transcendent theology could satisfy the demands of theoretical reason, and that such a system cannot be produced by the human intellect: "I can never *complete* the regress to the conditions of existence without assuming a *necessary* being, but I can never *begin* from such a being" (A616/B644). Schelling and Hegel both deny the adequacy of Kant's arguments in support of this contention, insisting that human reason can indeed construct an absolute system. Since Kant's most important argument on this point is to be found in his discussion of the "Ideal of Pure Reason," it makes a great deal of sense to say that that discussion contains the Kantian teaching crucial for the further development of German Idealism (see 11:283n). The different ways in which Schelling and Hegel attempt to avoid drawing the Kantian conclusion reveal the two fundamental options for establishing metaphysics in the wake of Kant.

It is in his presentation of the Ideal of Pure Reason, according to Schelling, that Kant establishes that the concept of the necessary being "is an idea that follows from the nature of reason itself and that is indispensable to every rational (*verstandesmässig*) determination of things" (11:284). According to Kant, every real entity must be fully determinate and thus must be, in principle if not in fact, fully conceptually determinable. It must be true that every possible predicate either applies or does not apply to every real entity; this must be true whether or not any intellect is capable of awareness of the application. At the same time, only an intellect that could make the complete determination could achieve complete theoretical satisfaction; only such an intellect could develop complete theoretical knowledge. The intellect that would know which predicates apply to which things would however first have to know—as a logical presupposition—"the aggregate (*Inbegriff*) of all predicates of things in general" (A572/B600). This aggregate of all possibility is termed by Kant an idea: it is fully concrete in that it must be taken to be fully determinate (A568/B596). In reflecting on the nature of this aggregate, the philosopher is not engaging in arbitrary speculation; he is, rather, considering an essential aspect of absolute knowledge.

Kant does not claim that philosophical reflection on the aggregate will lead to its complete construction; we are not, it would appear, capable of determining all the predicates that would belong therein. We can however exclude certain sorts of predicates from it. All concepts that are derived from other concepts can be excluded, as can, according to Kant, those "that cannot stand together," that is, those that contradict each other (A574/B602). Further reflection reveals that we can distinguish concepts that "represent a mere non-being" from those that express reality, and that, "no one can determinately think a negation without having grounded it in the opposed affirmation"; for this reason, all negative concepts can also be excluded. "All concepts of negations are derived, and the realities contain the data and, so to speak, tha matter, the transcendental content for the possibility and thorough determination of all things" (A575/B603). The aggregate would thus be "the idea of an entirety of reality (*omnitudo realitatis*)," but that is necessarily, according to Kant, the thought of a single perfect being. It is not merely concrete, it is individual, and thus appropriately named the Ideal of pure reason (A576/B604).

The aggregate of highest positive predicates is a thought that reason, considering what would satisfy its demands for knowledge, necessarily constructs. Whereas reason necessarily posits the idea, however, it has no warrant for positing that the Ideal—the entity to which the idea would correspond—actually exists (A577-78/B605-06). At the same time, it is natural—so natural as to be unavoidable—for reason to hypostatize the idea, thereby thinking God as existent (A580/B608). The hypostatization is not arbitrary, but neither is it justified. No only is it illicit to move from thought to existence, but furthermore, we are incapable of thinking God as determinate—of fully constructing the Idea—because our concepts are legitimately applicable only to things as they are sensibly experientiable, and God is unquestionably beyond the realm of sensible experience. We are not rationally justified, according to Kant, in claiming either that God exists or that we know what—in a conceptually determinate sense—he would be if he did exist. Because reason necessarily strives to unify its knowledge as systematically as possible, however, we are rationally required to reason as if determinate being were grounded in a single perfect, intelligent being, for that will facilitate our systematic consideration of the world itself (A672/B700).

Schelling agrees emphatically that the thought that the world is a rationally ordered whole entails the thought that the world is grounded in an absolute that is God—there can be wisdom rather than mere cleverness only if the stream of life is wisely ordered (see pp. 102–03 above)—and he frequently acknowledges that on this point Kant's influence has been cruical (13:45,79,91). He expresses the point most directly as a demand implied by the name "philosophy" itself:

> Philosophy means love of, striving for wisdom. Thus, not just any sort of knowledge will satisfy the philosopher, but only the knowledge that is wisdom. . . .
> If man demands a knowledge that is wisdom, he must presuppose that there is wisdom in the object of this knowledge. . . . There is no wisdom for man if there is none in the objective course of things. The first presupposition of philosophy as the striving for wisdom is thus that there is wisdom in . . . being, in the world itself. "I demand wisdom" means: I demand a [world] that has been posited wisely, providentially, freely (13:201-03).

Schelling agrees with Kant not only that reason demands God as absolute principle, but also that reason alone, unaided by experience, cannot determine whether or not God exists. Both Schelling and Kant reject the ontological proof in all of its forms, insisting that no thought or concept can alone establish the reality of an intelligent and benevolent deity.[5] According to Schelling, the ontological determination of the concept "God" reveals no more than that God can exist only as the absolute ground, that he must be that which is absolutely prior, the necessary being, if he exists (13:156-57; cf. 10:15-16).

The fact that God's existence could, in principle, be proved only *a posteriori* is, in Kant's view, one of three considerations indicating the impossibility of our grounding a metaphysical system in God. The second difficulty derives from our inability to even think the idea of God satisfactorily. As is indicated above, Kant denies that any of our concepts could legitimately be predicated of the absolute. Finally, Kant insists that in even attempting to think the notion of a primordial ground, an *Urgrund*, we discover only an abyss, an *Abgrund:*

> The unconditionally necessary [being] that we so indispensably require as the ultimate bearer of all things is the true abyss for reason. . . . The thought is as unbearable as it is unavoidable: that of the being that we represent to ourselves as the highest of all possible beings saying to itself, "I am from eternity to eternity, outside of me is nothing except that which is something through my will; *but from where, then, am I?*" Here, everything sinks beneath us, and the greatest perfection, like the least, wavers unsupported for speculative reason, which can, without losing anything, allow the one as well as the other, without the least hindrance, to disappear (A613/B642).

From the beginning of his philosophical career, Schelling regularly denies that there are difficulties in grounding God himself, in imagining "where God is from"; since the absolute is absolute, it must be from itself, it must be self-grounded in a primal reflection. The innovation crucial to positive philosophy—that whereby it surpasses the system of identity—relates to the first Kantian objection listed above rather than the third. Kant, having argued that God's existence could never be proved save through experience, proceeds to limit the scope of experience in such a way that it too is ruled out as a source of evidence relevant to the problem of God's existence: Kant restricts the experientiable to that which may be sensibly experienced, to that which may be directly perceived. It is with respect to the experientiable, and thus to the potential scope of empiricism, that Schelling diverges from Kant:

> It is a mistake to limit empiricism to the sensibly apparent (*Sinnenfällige*) as though that were its only object, in that, for example, a freely willing and acting intelligence, such as each of us is, does not as such, as intelligence, encounter the senses, and yet each is knowable empirically, indeed only empirically; for no one knows what is in a man if he does not express himself; with respect to his intellectual and moral character, he is knowable only *a posteriori*, through his expressions and acts. Assuming we were concerned with an acting, freely willing intelligence that was a presupposition for the existence of the world, that intelligence also would not be knowable *a priori*, but rather only through its deeds, deeds that would be visible in the realm of experience; it would thus, although supersensible, be knowable only through experience. Empiricism as such thus by no means excludes all knowledge of the supersensible. . . . (13:113; cf. *GPP*:95).

The remaining Kantian objection to the grounding of a system in God concerns the applicability of our concepts to what is not sensibly accessible. This limitation of our determinative abilities is taken no more seriously by Schelling than by Fichte or Hegel, largely because all were convinced that Kant himself had successfully surpassed it: Kant's transcendental consideration of the intellect is completely dependent on non-sensible access to its object, and is expressible only through concepts that—according to the principle that would deny that we can determine the idea of God—should be applicable only within the realm of sensible experience.

If Kant and Schelling are right in arguing (1) that the philosopher would be fully satisfied only by becoming completely certain that the world is wisely ordered, (2) that that requires metaphysical grounding in God, and (3) that God's existence could be proved only through reliance on experience, then Schelling's "philosophical" or "metaphysical empiricism" (13:114) must play a crucial role in the true philosophical system.[6] Schelling frequently indicates that role by expressing his project in the form of a hypothetical syllogism. The major premise states that if the finite world is grounded in God, then it must have the characteristics x, y, and z. The first systematic task is that of determining what x, y, and z would follow from God; this is the task of a negative philosophy[7], negative in that it must be accomplished *a priori*, in thought alone, and thus has access only to the possible, not to the actual (see 11:297–99,321).

The minor premise of Schelling's syllogism asserts that x, y, and z are present in the world as experienced. This premise could be conclusively established as true only if the world as a whole, in the entirety of its historical development, were accessible. Since it is not—and could not be, at least until it has been completed—analyses of the factical world—*a posteriori*, empirical analyses that are "positive" in that they deal with the truly existent—can only make the premise appear increasingly probable.

The conclusion of the philosophical syllogism is, of course, that God exists as ground of the world (13:129,169; cf. 14:346, *GPP*:115-17, 401). The syllogism, as Schelling presents it, is formally invalid, but that is not systematically important, for Schelling actually attempts to show that x, y, and z could be present *only* if the world is grounded in God, and his conclusion does follow necessarily if that premise is established.[8] At the same time, however, Schelling does not claim that his arguments are absolutely compelling: since the syllogism's minor premise cannot be established, neither can its conclusion. Philosophy is not to be transformed into wisdom; it will rather remain *philo-sophia*. The philosopher will continue to examine the "fact of the world" as it has unfolded and as it further unfolds, seeking the traces he knows must be visible therein if the world is in fact grounded in God (13:131).

The project of Schelling's final system, as expressed in the syllogism, is structurally identical to that of the *System of Transcendental Idealism* of 1800. In each, *a priori* constructions are developed and then tested against the reality of the experienced world. The tests are, however, intended to serve quite different purposes. In the 1800 *System*, correspondence with the world is the criterion for the adequacy of the construction itself; the purpose of the comparison is the determination of the stringency with which the philosopher has been able to adhere to the method. For the finite constructions of that system, such a test would make sense. If I construct, for example, magnetism, I can then examine the experienced world to determine whether the construct corresponds to the reality.

Within the context of positive philosophy, experience still functions as the control proving that reason's *finite* constructions are not chimerical, that they do correspond to structures and entities in the factical world. But, according to Schelling, the philosopher knows in advance that if anything at all exists, then the reality must agree with the construction. Experience shows that there is something rather than nothing. Reason alone has no access to existence, but it has complete access to essence. The construction, as purely essential, can be adequately tested by reason alone and, to the extent that it satisfies reason's purely logical requirements, it would, Schelling insists, be true even if nothing existed (13:162-63,128-29).

The greatest concern of the positive philosopher is not, however, proof of the existence of sensibly experientiable things, but rather proof of the existence of God. Since God can never be an entity simply and straightforwardly visible within the factical world, the simple correspondence test of the 1800 *System* is inadequate for this most important case. With respect to God's existence, Schelling's indirect empirical proof is the only one possible: if the real world corresponds in certain crucial respects to the philosophical construct, then we should conclude, albeit not with certainty, that God exists.

Like the physico-theological proof, Schelling's syllogism attempts to ground the conviction that God exists in features of the experienced world; but it is important that the two proofs not be confused. Not only has Kant argued that the physico-theological proof presupposes the ontological proof, which Schelling rejects. Furthermore, according to Schelling, it is illicit to move simply from that which is actually posterior—the world—to that which is prior. Rather than thus reasoning from consequent to antecedent, Schelling reasons from absolute spirit to the world, first determining—albeit "negatively"—what would follow from absolute spirit as ground. Positive philosophy is, with respect to the world, an *a priori* science, starting from the very beginning—the absolute *prius*—and deriving determinations from it in the original order. With respect to the complete absolute spirit, however, it is an *a posteriori* science, "in that it proves the existence of that spirit, it explains or is the science of that spirit, only by examining what is posterior to it" (13:249).

CREATION, MYTH, REVELATION

The negative construction with which the positive philosophical system begins retains the fundamental features of the dialectic of the system of identity. For this reason, the positive system as a whole may be accurately described as the true transfiguration of the system of identity first projected in the *Freedom* essay (7:333-35). In seeking to retain parts of that system, however, Schelling retains some of its most vexing problems. Central is one that plagues him throughout his career, the problem of creation, of the descent from infinite to finite:

> if I do not grasp (*einsehe*) how a being thought as outside of the world and exalted above it could produce a world different from and posited outside of itself, then this presupposition could perhaps arouse my faith, even influence my life, but I would have insight into nothing more than mere words that would not be understood (13:42).

The construction of the absolute itself, independent of the finite, is handled by Schelling with typical facility: he continues to argue that reason's demands for grounds can be satisfied only if its regress ends with a being that grounds its own existence in an act of self-reflection. The three moments distinguished in the act—the absolute as subject, as object, and as subject–object (the unity of the first two)—are those introduced in the system of identity as the primal "powers" A, B, and A^2. In the context of positive philosophy, Schelling characterizes and develops the moments in various ways. He occasionally uses A's and B's (e.g. 13:355-56), but also names the moments "being in itself, for itself, and with itself (*bei sich*)" (e.g. 11:289-91) and, in modal terminology, "that which can be, that which must be, and that which shall be (*das Seynkönnende, das Seynmüssende, das Seynsollende*) (e.g. 13:267). The moments are also related to the Platonic–Pythagorean principles of unlimited, limited, and determinate being (11:393,12:112–3, 13:342). The terminological variety indicates Schelling's conviction that his distinction is extremely important, yet the variety leads to ambiguity rather than to clarity.[9] More helpful than the abstract terms is Schelling's continuing reliance on the fundamental structure of reflection. This structure is now explicitly related to the traditional notion of God as trinity, most directly to Leibniz's teaching concerning the latter (13:315). In Schelling's words,

> Self-consciousness is thinkable only if at least three internal distinctions are posited. That which is self-conscious is (1) that which is conscious of itself, (2) that of which it is itself conscious, and because the latter is not an other, outside of the former, but is rather one and the same with it, it can thus be thought *tertio loco* as that which is *self-conscious* (13:73-74).

Nothing less than conviction that the world is grounded in such an absolute could, according to Schelling, satisfy the demands of reason; since this absolute would originate in a spiritual act—that of self-reflection—the demand is that the world be grounded in absolute spirit (13:239). As absolute, Schelling insists, this spirit is thought as complete and self-sufficient; thus, the finite cannot follow from it with any sort of logical necessity. In attempting to develop a teaching that will present the creation as other than necessary, Schelling first suggests that, at the very least, the possibility of creation cannot be excluded from the absolute that has been constructed (12:39). Spirit, as absolute, can have no need to create, but it has not been posited as either unwilling or unable to create (13:263-64). Nothing prevents us, Schelling continues, from imagining this possibility "showing itself" to spirit without thereby being actualized by it: the powers would, in this manifestation, beome visible as potential principles for a non-absolute being (13:267). Spirit is not bound to actualize the possibility, but Schelling suggests that the possibility will be attractive in that it provides the opportunity for free expression. Independent of this opportunity, spirit simply is as it is—it has not willed that it be so. If it wills the actualization of the powers, it will have acted as absolute, it will not merely be absolute. Indeed, once the possibility "shows itself," spirit must in a certain sense act freely: it must choose either to create or not to create. Furthermore, now that we have seen that absolute spirit must be thought as positively free— at least if it is to be able to serve as ground for finite being—rather than as merely non-compelled, we must recognize that we have thought absolute spirit as God (13:269).

This emphasis on the importance of a divine choice signals an important development in Schelling's doctrine of divine freedom. In his earliest writings, that freedom is always presented as the absolute freedom that is equivalent to absolute necessity: action in accordance with essence (rather than action under external influence or compulsion). According to the later Schelling, neither creation nor non-creation is determined by a divine essence: "God is bound to nothing, not even to his own being" (13:305). If God were so bound, creation would have to be envisioned as a logically necessary emanation; if creation were necessary, however, God's divinity would be dependent upon the existence of the world. Schelling agrees with Newton that *Deus est vox relativa* in that he is master of the world; for Schelling, however, he is the true master in that he is free to posit the world or not, as he chooses (13:291). Earlier philosophers were, according to Schelling, forced to resort to doctrines of emanation—and thus, eventually, to the affirmation of a complete metaphysical necessity— by their failure to discover a middle term between God and his creative act. In Schelling's doctrine, the mediating position is held by God's awareness of the possibility of creation; this possibility is "the first object of divine knowledge" (13:293); in it, God sees "the prologue of the entire future world," he sees the ideas, the "eternal models of things" (13:293-94; cf. *GPP*:448).

In essence, the first claim in Schelling's creation doctrine is that the possibility of creation cannot simply be excluded from the absolute. An account of any actual creation must however answer two further questions: that of how creation will work if God wills it, and that of why God might will it (13:271). Concerning the second, Schelling first asserts that God, in his pure absoluteness, is not yet truly articulated: the three moments have not become persons, they are not truly distinct. Furthermore, the unity of the absolute purely as such is so complete that—as Schelling also teaches in his earliest writings—there is therein no self-knowledge (13:273-74); if God is to know himself, he can come to do so only through the complete self-reflection that will allow the moments to develop as distinct powers (13:274). A second explanation of the reason for creation, "less clever but fully relevant," would hold that God cannot will the finite for his own sake since he is in need of nothing; he must therefore will it, if at all, for the sake of something that would result, a creature (13:277)—and if for the sake of a creature, then for one that will be able to appreciate his generosity, a fully self-conscious creature such as man (13:287; 12:109, 118; 14:351-52; *GPP*:469).

Whatever the reason, God may create if he decides to do so. Since the creation will not be an emanation, it is best described, according to Schelling, as a begetting or generation (*Zeugung*) (13:312). If the creative possibility is allowed to actualize, then the first moment will become a power independent of the other two:

> that which [in the abstract idea of the trinity] is merely the being in itself can raise itself, can go over into an objective being outside of itself. The peculiarity and the true strength of my idea lies in the claim that that being in itself contains the matter, the occasion (*Veranlassung*), the possibility for a tension [among the three moments]. It is this aspect of my idea that insures its lasting influence on science; for thereby, that unity becomes living, self-moving, and there becomes visible at least the possibility of moving from it to three powers that exclude each other—to a true life (13:316).

The begetting—the positing of a tension among the powers—is a negation of the primordial unity, but not a permanent one; the purpose of the process is not the negation itself, but rather the eventual negation of that negation (13:325).

The process of purely divine creation is eternal and, although moments are distinguishable as prior and posterior, the relations are logical rather than temporal (14:356), the creation ideal rather than real. The ideal process is complete when there arises a being that shares God's completeness in being the same unity of powers, and in being, like God, bound to none; this being with whom the tension is overcome is, of course, man in his primordial form (13:344-46,118). Since he is like God rather than like any one of the powers, man is also capable of allowing a tension to arise among the powers. In his primordial form, man is above the powers—he contains them in equilibrium—but he is not yet ruler of them, since they have not yet, for him, become actualized as distinct. He does not however realize that this "not yet" indicates a crucial difference between his position and God's: "He imagines that he can be master of the powers in their separation just as he is master of them in their original unity. Precisely therein lies the great if nearly unavoidable illusion (*Täuschung*)" (13:349; cf. 12:19-21).

Schelling thus reasserts a fundamental teaching of "Philosophy and Religion" and of the *Freedom* essay: in attempting to become fully like God, as real master of the content implicit in the powers, man falls. He thereby frees the first moment from his control; it can be subdued—the unity of powers can be restored—only through a temporal process. The general developmental structure of the process will, indeed, be determined by the powers, and not by man—who has lost control of them—or by God, who is fully articulated and completely stable as of the end of the ideal process.[10] Since the development is structured by the powers, it can be rationally—negative-philosophically—reconstructed (13:359,359n). The question crucial to positive philosophy is that of which features of the reconstructed world would, if also present in the existent world, provide evidence that the latter really does have its origin in man's attempt to become fully like God.[11]

If the real creation is grounded in man's willful fall—as it must be if man himself is ultimately grounded in God—then man's fundamental desire within the finite realm must be that of mastering the powers by positing them as the primal spiritual unity—God—in and through which all would be rational. The attempted positing is not, however, a matter simply of theoretical construction: the powers exist, and are separate, so the mere positing of them as united would not lead to true mastery of them. The powers are involved in a temporal process and they must be really, not merely ideally, unified. Their unification cannot be immediately accomplished: the first principle, the source of irrationality, attempts to retain the autonomy man has given it, it resists the efforts of the second, rational power to know it.[12] As long as it retains this autonomy—as it must throughout the first epoch of the historical process—the ruling principle of the world is indeed the dark, irrational power, and man's attempts to mythically posit it as such result from his own accurate insight into the state of the world as it is, and not from any philosophical, scientific, or religious naiveté. As long as the irrational principle is completely predominant, man will see the world—if he sees it correctly—as governed by a single unintelligible god. As the second power gains in strength, leading to conflict and development, theogonic myths will express the truth of the situation. Finally, with the development in which the rational principle comes to have real ascendency over the irrational such that the two are united while remaining distinct, man will be able to posit the true trinitarian monotheism, the truly Christian religion.

Prior to relating his dialectical powers directly to mythic gods in order to support his central contention that the two are the same, Schelling attempts to reveal the explicatory necessity of the contention in the "historical–critical" introduction to the Philosophy of Mythology. There he argues that traditional theories—according to which myths are grounded in poetry, or are best understood as primitive forms of either natural science or rational philosophy—fail to explain the phenomenon. Summarizing the conclusions of that argument in the *Revelation* lectures, he insists that "these representations—the mythological ones—cannot be explained in any other way [save my own], as the results of all previous hypotheses have clearly shown; they cannot be explained as invented (*erfundene*), not as imagined (*erdichtete*), not as resulting either from a merely contingent confusion or from a prior revelation; they are, rather, thinkable only as necessary products of the fallen human consciousness that is under the dominion of the powers that themselves, in their separation, have lost their divine significance, and have become merely cosmic" (13:378; cf. 11:125). This argument supports the valid form of the Schellingian syllogism: it contends that *only* if the absolute is God can the "*x* and *y*" of myth follow.

The theogonic process itself will be at once ideal and, in a specific sense, real:

> In the mythological process, man is not involved with things; the process is rather animated by the forces that arise within consciousness itself. The theogonic process through which mythology arises is subjective in that it advances within consciousness and makes itself known through the projection of representations: but the causes and thus also the objects of these representations are the actual theogonic forces, the forces in themselves, precisely the same ones through which consciousness is existent as positing God. The content of the process is not merely represented powers, it is the powers themselves—the ones that produce consciousness and, since consciousness is only the end of nature, that also produce nature, and that are thus actual forces. The mythological process has nothing to do with natural objects, but with the pure productive powers, whose primordial product is consciousness itself. It is here, then, that the explanation enters the objective realm, and thus becomes fully objective itself (11:207; cf. 13:379,500-01).

The positive philosopher's understanding of the principles, the powers, allows him to identify the necessity underlying the superficial diversity among the mythic productions of various societies:

> ... the principle according to which mythology develops is the principle of a successive stepping forth (*Hervortreten*) of the powers that were united in primordial consciousness, and that reunite themselves only successively. . . the entire mythological process revolves around the three powers. They are what is essential in the process, and insofar as they appear to consciousness as gods then, as I have said before,

only those gods that enter consciousness successively are the truly causal, the essential gods (13:396).

Schelling's theory allows for contingent aspects within the history of myth; he retains the argument of the *Freedom* essay according to which the functionality of the irrational principle insures that there will be irrational and contingent features present in the factical world; metaphysical necessity no longer reigns absolute.

The method of the Philosophy of Mythology corresponds to the structure expressed in Schelling's philosophical syllogism. Following the rational determination of what the theogonic process would be and how it would develop, Schelling proceeds to the "Philosophy of Mythology itself," that is, "the demonstration, through mythology, of the actuality of such a (theogonic) movement of consciousness" (14:10). In fact, the negative and positive developments—the rational and the historical investigations— are presented together: rather than completing his account of the former before beginning the latter, Schelling exhibits each step historically as soon as it has been constructed rationally. He does not fail, however, to stress the methodological priority of the rational. Steps are first "derived from the inner workings of the mythological development itself" and then "demonstrated in fact, historically" (12:252; cf. 12:257,13:464-65,513).[13]

The theogonic process is thus presented as the process through which the divine powers—which have, as a result of the fall, become "merely cosmic"—reconstruct the articulated but unified configuration in which they stand within the divine unity. The theogonic process visible in myth is both necessary and true in that it reflects the development of the powers—"Polytheism, considered in the totality of its successive moments, is the way to truth and to that extent is itself truth" (12:212)—and in that it ends with an accurate image of the triune God. Yet myth, the counterpart to the wholly necessary, rationally accessible interplay of the powers, cannot reveal the true relation of the God it so imagines to human beings and to the world (12:212): mythic consciousness does not become aware of why there is something rather than nothing; it cannot determine why God created the world.

For the philosopher, awareness of the theogonic process, even in its necessity, cannot alone explain why this awareness is possible, why human consciousness retains sufficient unity that it is not simply destroyed by its own attempt to become fully like God. According to Schelling, it is intelligible that man is not thereby destroyed only if God himself, having realized that man would fall if given the chance, decided nonetheless to reveal himself to man in the process (14:8-9). *Because* the truth is finally revealed to man, we can know that God originally decided to create *for the sake* of man. This then is the answer to the question, "why is there something rather than nothing?" If there were no such answer, then philosophy would be impossible, for there would be no wisdom "in the world itself":

> There must be a *finis quaerendi et inveniendi*, a goal at which the never-resting spirit rests; for otherwise all knowledge would be in vain, that is, pointless. There must arise something in the development of things where human knowledge, which has in itself an infinite drive towards progress and movement, must confess that it can proceed no further, where it thus becomes silent (14:27).

The truth with which man can rest is revealed in Christian teachings, after the theogonic process has been completed. But this is not to say that the Christian Bible is an authority the philosopher simply accepts. Rather,

> ... the reality—this is to be well noted—the reality of the principles that make revelation conceivable (*aus welchen sich die Offenbarung begreift*) has been confirmed for us, independently of revelation, through the mammoth appearance of mythology. This is the role of the Philosophy of Mythology within a Philosophy of Revelation (13:530).

The status of "revelation" as a source of knowledge *distinct from reason* is established, according to Schelling, by the demonstration that man has accurate evidential access to the cosmic powers through myth: "A real relation of the human essence to God is verified by the Philosophy of Mythology prior to all revelation, and grounded on so broad a basis that I may assume it as firmly and unshakably established" (14:29). Man's relation to God is real rather than merely ideal in that his access to God is not primarily rational (cf. 13:142-44,150-52). Even at the historical point where truth becomes fully accessible—where the powers have achieved a state of balance correspondent to that within the divine unity—it is at first grasped only by a privileged few, who must inform others. Since access to the principles and to God is not, at that point, through reason, intelligence is not a factor in determining who the few will be (see esp. 10:17).

The truth finally revealed in the Christian teaching—fundamentally, through the person of Jesus Christ (e.g., 14:232)—is that there is something rather than nothing because God decided to allow man to become fully and self-consciously one with himself, even knowing that because man would originally act pridefully the full oneness could be stably present only following a finite temporal process. In accordance with the doctrine of temporality first developed in the unpublished *Ages of the World*, the stable unity is the state of the "eternal future" that will follow the world-process as a whole; the latter is established as a true cosmic "present" through its relation to that future, and to the "eternal past," the primordial state of unity established as *past* by man, in and through his fall from it. Because God did not forsake man when man forsook God, the two will be reunited in the post-temporal future.

This Christian truth is, according to Schelling, the truth that reveals the presence of "wisdom in the world." With respect to this truth, the philosopher is not primarily concerned with interpreting the writings of the few apostles to whom the truth was originally revealed; rather, revealed religion must give way to "philosophical religion," which is to be grounded in a knowledge "that would be possible for and accessible to human beings under all circumstances, at all times and in all places, that is, universal human knowledge, as free, scientific knowledge" (14:296). Schelling's positive philosophy is presented as providing the theoretical ground for this "truly spiritual house of God. . . in which all human striving, willing, thinking, and knowing would be brought into complete unity" (14:296).

Schelling does not directly consider the first two aspects of this unity—striving and willing—because, he asserts, "the practical, the moral [aspects] of Christian life follow of themselves from the theoretical ideas" (14:293). Since however Schelling insists—in opposition to Hegel—that only a theological metaphysics can provide the basis for the avoidance of nihilism, the possibilities for the expansion of positive philosophy to include the practical realm must be considered.

THEORY AND PRACTICE

The late Schelling's practical teachings are revealed most fully in an introductory argument in the "Exhibition of Pure Rational Philosophy" designed to establish that the various possible ways in which human beings attempt to attain satisfaction reveal their deficiencies in such a way that positive philosophy remains as the sole option. Having argued that although man completes nature merely by existing, he is not originally complete in himself, Schelling proceeds to the consideration of human attempts to achieve fulfillment. Since it is humanity as a whole—rather than any specific individual—that completes nature, Schelling begins by treating the order and organization of mankind. The rational order for the whole—an order both racial and political—is fully concrete in the realm of ideas (11:530; cf. 506) and, although man as actual no longer has complete access to the ideas, their traces are visible in the finite world:

> The rational order as external and armed with forcing power is the state, which is, materially considered, a mere fact having only factical existence, but which is sanctified by the law that lives in it, a law that has its source not in this world or in man, but rather immediately in the intelligible world. The law that has become factical power is the answer to the deed through which man places himself outside of reason; this is reason in history (11:533).

Though this passage suggests that an extant just state would restore the unity destroyed in man's fall, that solution is not, according to Schelling, a real possibility. The ideal ground of the state is fully rational but, partly because this ground tends to be invisible to individuals, and partly because contingencies—and therefore irrationalities—cannot be excluded from the constitution of any real state (11:538), the individual feels that his freedom is limited by the state's laws (11:534-35). To an extent, the subject's freedom is in fact enhanced within the state for, as subjected to its laws, the human being becomes accountable for his deeds: he becomes, in Schelling's terms, a person rather than a mere individual (11:536). Nevertheless, since the person's convictions concerning what is right must at least occasionally conflict with the laws of the state, the philosopher must conclude that the political realm is not one in which he can find ultimate fulfillment. The individual should avoid being constrained by the state, then, not by opposing it politically, but by being internally beyond its reach (11:547-48). Schelling embraces the Platonic teaching that the philosopher loses very little in forsaking the political arena; even if a state were ideal, political duties within it would distract the philosopher from higher, more important things (11:549).

Because the political realm is a merely finite one, the Schellingian philosopher is not concerned with political progress (11:550). At the same time, however, Schelling assures his audience that such progress is of the order of things, that it will come of itself (11:551; cf. 13:10). Be that as it may, the philosopher realizes that he can become truly moral, and truly satisfied, only within himself, only as individual and not as person: his primary responsibility is thus to himself (11:553). Hence, he isolates himself from the real, turning to a search for an inner infinitude—according to Schelling, for a God that he does not yet know. In thus denying himself he reacquires the contact with God that he lost following his original fall (11:556). He thereby gains at least the idea of God, and attempts to strengthen it through further self-denial, through art, and finally through pure contemplation (11:558-59). He finds a complacency in his meditations—on, apparently, "the idea of God"—but as soon as his physical needs force him to return to the practical domain, his equanimity is lost; the end of his purely rational attempt to attain satisfaction is a to-tal skeptical despair. At this point, there are only two options: either the nihilism with which rational inquiry ends must be accepted, or the philosopher must posit his idea of God, which has arisen for him only as an end, as an absolute beginning: if he does the latter, determining then what would follow from God as absolute ground, he has entered the realm of positive philosophy.

The process of positive philosophy itself has already been considered, but the task left for the post-Schellingian philosopher has not. Although Schelling insists that philosophy is to remain *philo-sophia*—that it is not to be transformed into wisdom—he also takes himself to have completed positive philosophy to as complete an extent as is possible, at least in his historical epoch; it is only after that completion that he returns to the negative-philosophical investigations that culminate with the "Exhibition of Pure Rational Philosophy." Even if there was no positive-philosophical work left for Schelling, however, it might be suspected that his successors would be provided by the development of history with phenomena that would require philosophical interpretation. Yet, according to Schelling, the period of divine revelation has come to an end; it is, in his time, as possible as it ever will be to determine rationally that the world is grounded in God, and revealed religion will be supplanted by philosophical religion, it would seem, as soon as Schelling's teachings are assimilated by the public. Schelling thus does not teach that what will happen "next" in the temporal realm is of the utmost importance; the focus is rather on the eternal "ages" of past and future, in the context of which alone the finite present—within which all truly is vanity—has any meaning or value.

Schelling's final concern is thus by no means with "changing the world," despite the emphasis of his opening lectures (see pp. 93–97 above). In addition, whereas those first lectures establish the importance of attributing to man an immanent and effective freedom and power—if man were merely pushed around by the stream into which he is thrown, he would be no more than a dead object—the stress throughout the lectures is on human impotence, on man's inability to change the world or to influence the course of history. We are thrown into a stream and, Schelling's teachings indicate, we can be truly satisfied only if it is a good stream—only then can we happily subject ourselves to its forces. We are accorded some degree of autonomy, but that autonomy is not explained, and it is so limited that it seems to be a defect rather than a perfection: according to Schelling, we control only our own acts, we remain totally powerless with respect to their consequences. Our apprehension in the face of the unknown consequences must be so great, he continues, that we can bring ourselves to perform great deeds only if we are convinced in advance that the results are ordered providentially—only if, again, we believe that the course the stream will in any case take is a good one (13:116; see 3:597-600).

Schelling's "practical" teaching, to the extent that such exists, is grounded in his conviction that man is fundamentally impotent; his assertion—one often made in the works of his youth[14]—that the practical follows clearly from the theoretical, so that no distinct practical teaching is required, is made little more attractive by his assurances that political progress is unavoidable—the result of what might as well be a blind metaphysical necessity. If the world is to change, he teaches, it will change, but rational human activity will have no real role in the process.

The positive philosopher is thus left with nothing to do—practice, having been subordinated to contemplation, never reacquires real importance—and with nothing really to think about save perhaps the intellectually intuited idea of God. Schelling himself was no mystic—he was obsessed throughout his life with analyzable facts and appearances of all sorts, natural, spiritual, and textual—but the only activity left for one who has comprehended his teachings would seem to be the mystic's meditation on an idea that is beyond all discursive articulation. At the end of the positive development, then, the philosopher is returned to the point of culmination of negative philosophy, where there is satisfaction in contemplation, but where the necessity of practical activity continues to bring with it the threat of skeptical—nihilistic—despair. The claim that theoretical understanding of what is brings with it practical enlightenment concerning what should be done in specific cases is, finally, evidence of

Schelling's lifelong lack of interest in practical problems, not the result of serious consideration of them. He fails to make the transition from theory to practice; he does not banish the specter of nihilism.

In failing to make the step from theory to practice, positive philosophy fails to satisfy Schelling's requirements for its success. Even if a practical doctrine were appended, however, Schelling's final system would remain far from satisfactory. First, Schelling never solves a problem that he acknowledges to be crucial within his system: the problem of the descent from infinite to finite. God's "vision of the possibility of a creation" is far too obscure to have any explanatory value as the middle term between God and the world. Second, the dialectic of powers is fundamentally identical to that of Schelling's early system. Hegel criticizes its empty formalism as early as 1807, in the Preface to the *Phenomenology*. Schelling himself insists "that anything that can be expressed only in a contorted and confused manner cannot, for just that reason, be the true and the right" (13:19; 14:58). The polemics against obscure formulations are directed against Hegel, but they could certainly be applied to the doctrine of powers—which, according to Kierkegaard, wholly disillusioned after three months of Schelling's lectures, "reveals the greatest impotence."[15]

A third point of difficulty for positive philosophy concerns its relation to religion. While denying that he desires to establish any sort of religious dogma (14:30,293) and insisting that his attempt to understand the significance of Christ is methodologically identical to his attempt to grasp the true importance of such purely mythic figures as Dionysus (14:201; cf. 13:133-40), Schelling at times seems to assert that Christian doctrine could have arisen historically only if Jesus Christ actually existed as the son of God. While we have no reason to assume or even suspect that the gods of the heathens were "historical persons," the situation with respect to Christ is quite different: "he lived like other men, he was born and he died, and his historical existence is as fully documented (*beglaubigt*) as that of any other historical person" (14:229-30). The birth of Christ, as the son of God, "at a determinate time" is a final but fully external event, one entirely within the sphere of other phenomena (*Begebenheiten*). This fact could not come forth merely in the consciousness of humanity; unlike the facts of myth, it could not have a merely subjectively objective (*subjektiv-objektiv*) truth; for it an absolutely objective truth was necessary, it had to be something that occurred independently of human representations (14:173).

Schelling comes quite close to teaching that the appearance of Jesus Christ, as a historical person, is proof of determinate divine intervention in the historical process; yet his principles certainly do not allow him to present such a teaching, for it would draw God himself into the temporal process, negating his absoluteness. Schelling's principles would allow only the teaching that the representation of the son of God as existent is possible only if God has preserved the unity of human spirit despite the fall which should otherwise have destroyed that unity. This latter teaching, which would not introduce an inconsistency into the system, might suffice; yet closer consideration of the architectonic of the development indicates that the introduction of Christ is a crucial as well as a difficult point. The development of the powers to which the development of myth corresponds could lead only to an equilibrium point where the first two powers were contained within the third; for the quantum jump to revelation, Schelling requires a fourth, beyond the powers, a higher unity analogous to what God necessarily is and to what man once was—master of the three powers. The new transcendent entity that alone could mediate between God and man would have to be both "fully God and fully man" and, for this role, Jesus Christ is obviously the leading candidate. Nevertheless, Schelling's insistence on the absoluteness of the absolute, of the completeness of God following the ideal creation, would seem to exclude the possibility of a divine presence in or influence on the finite process.

To do justice to a philosopher, Schelling insists, one must identify and evaluate his fundamental thought (13:60). Schelling's own fundamental thought is that there issues, from the primal self-reflection of an indeterminate absolute, a real process that is reconstructible, at least in outline, by the philosopher. This thought is exhaustively criticized by Hegel in the Logic of Essence. As I have attempted to show elsewhere,[16] the changes in Schelling's system following the appearance of Hegel's major works cannot be understood as attempts to avoid Hegel's objections to the system of identity, for Schelling in fact simply ignores those objections. Schelling is forced to change his system rather because of defects he had himself recognized: he was determined to produce a system of freedom—a system grounding human beings as free—but was forced to acknowledge that the system of identity is a system of necessity.[17] In that positive philosophy remains rooted in the same fundamental thought, however, it does not represent a step beyond Hegel.

Kant insists that the demands of human reason would be satisfied only by transcendent metaphysical knowledge we cannot acquire: "I can never complete the regress to the conditions of existence without assuming a necessary being, but I can never begin from such a being" (A:616/B:644). Schelling agrees concerning the demands of reason, and attempts to surpass Kant by deriving what is from a primal absolute entity; the failure of his attempt serves however only to confirm the contention of Kant—and Hegel—that such a derivation is impossible. If there is to be a post-Kantian metaphysics that satisfies the traditional requirements of first philosophy, it cannot be fundamentally theological: it cannot start with God, for theology cannot become ontology. Hegel's ontological option is thus the only one that has a chance of success.

6

Hegelian Wisdom

PHILOSOPHY AND CONTINGENCY

Positive philosophy is introduced above as Schelling's attempt to put Kant's doctrine of the Ideal of Pure Reason to constructive theological use: Schelling accepts Kant's line of reasoning up to the point where Kant denies that empirical evidence for the proof of God's existence is available, but then attempts to surpass Kant through the development of his "metaphysical empiricism." This is the general course that any post-Kantian metaphysical theology must take. Hegel does not take this course; he attempts instead to ground a non-theological first philosophy, a transcendental ontology. Hegel's reflective step from Kant's critical standpoint to the speculative one may, like Schelling's, be understood as resulting from the attempt to utilize Kant's doctrine of the Ideal, but Hegel diverges from Kant far earlier in the course of argumentation: he disagrees concerning the idea of the "aggregate of all predicates of things in general," prior to the point where the idea is hypostatized as the Ideal.

Kant, it will be remembered, purifies the idea, reducing it to "the idea of an entirety of reality (*omnitudo realitatis*)" that reason tends to hypostatize as God; Hegel objects to the process of purification. Kant excludes from the idea first all mutually exclusive concepts, and then all concepts that express negations; Hegel's *Logic* attempts to demonstrate that both exclusions are, strictly speaking, impossible (see *L2:61/SL:442*). Hegel would by no means deny that only one of two contradictories can apply to

143

anything in a single respect; yet, he insists, concepts can be applied at all only if they are themselves determinate, and no concept can be concretely understood in isolation from its opposite. The same holds with respect to Kant's second exclusion: Hegel denies that positive conceptes are truly intelligible in isolation from correlated negations. Kant presents negative concepts as "derivative," but, Hegel argues, they can be "derived" from their positive correlates only because they are ingredient in them: "presence," for example, is meaningless save as opposed to "absence."

Having denied the legitimacy of the Kantian exclusions, Hegel proceeds with the derivation of the aggregate of fundamental determinations, completing it with—and as—the Absolute Idea. The naming of the categorial network as a whole "Idea" rather than "Ideal" is a further indication that Hegel's concern is not with a transcendent absolute. Since the "idea of possible predicates" never, according to Hegel, becomes that of an "entirety of reality" exclusive of negatives and contradictories, there is no possibility of—and there should thus be no temptation to—its hypostatization as an entity whose existence could be an important philosophical issue.

If the Absolute Idea is not intended to be a transcendent entity, then, according to Schelling, the crucial philosophical problem Hegel cannot solve is that of nihilism. This claim is grounded in the argument that philosophy, as the love of wisdom, demands that the world be wisely ordered, and that that order provide a rational basis for the distinction between right and wrong. For Schelling, the world is wisely ordered only if its course is directed by God. hegel disagrees with Schelling on three fundamental points.

Hegel disagrees, first, with Schelling's insistence that the philosopher must demand, prior to concrete investigation, that the world be ordered in accordance with wisdom and justice. On this point, Hegel remains true to Fichte's teaching that the philosopher's "highest maxim" demands "that he seek only the truth, however it may be," so that "even the truth that there is no truth would be welcome to him, if that were indeed the truth."[1] Fichte's footnote becomes the famous Hegelian dictum, "Philosophy must avoid wanting to be edifying" (*PG*:14/*PS*:6). This is not to say that Hegel's teachings will not be edifying in the end, that they are indeed powerless in the face of a growing tendency to nihilism; it is only to say that the development of an ethical or religious doctrine that will correspond to what common consciousness holds to be the right, the good, and the desirable is not the primary end of Hegelian philosophy.

Schelling insists that because Hegel's is a science of pure thought, it must fail with respect to practical philosophy. Pure thought has access, according to Schelling, only to two realms: the purely essential realms of the possible and the necessary. Pure thought can develop, at best, accounts of what can be but need not be, and of what cannot be otherwise. The exhaustive cosmological science of these realms is, in Schelling's view, his own negative philosophy, wherein an account is given of what will be— necessarily—if anything at all is. The ontological account of the merely possible could be, according to Schelling, no more than a presentation of the concepts abstracted from the actual, the existent; the ontological science of the necessary would have as its content only the tautologously apodictic, it could consider only the sort of empty identities—those having the form "$A = A$"— that Hegel himself rejects as fully indeterminate and thus uninteresting.[2] Be those accounts as they may, Schelling continues, the ontologist cannot possibly provide an account of the contingent, of what, though it need not be, nonetheless is. Hegel, as transcendental ontologist, must ignore philosophy's most important subject matter:

> The world does not consist of mere categories or pure concepts, it does not consist of concrete concepts, but rather of concrete and contingent things, and the matter at hand is the illogical, the other, which is not the concept but its opposite, which only unwillingly accepts the concept. It is here that philosophy is put to the test (*GPP*:225).

Schelling's insistence on the philosophical importance of the merely contingent is the second claim with which Hegel is in flat disagreement: according to Hegel, "the contingent is an existent that has no greater value than that of the possible, which, although it is, might just as well not be" (*E*:§6A). As is indicated above, Hegel's doctrine of truth teaches that judgments reporting only what happens to be are at best merely correct; they cannot express the truth with which the philosopher is concerned. The philosopher therefore does not focus on what is or what happens as such. He seeks rather to determine the aspects of the contingent that are merely contingent; he aims to reveal those that are also true. In Hegel's view, those who value the knowledge of what merely takes place as the most important philosophical knowledge remain fixated at the standpoint that should have been overcome through Kant's "Copernican revolution": they continue to view the object, rather than the determinations of thought, as the ground of truth. For Hegel, philosophy tests reality to determine the extent to which it is true; reality is incapable of testing the truths of philosophy.

Hegel's science is fundamentally that of the determinations of thought that could not be otherwise: the Absolute Idea is presented as the aggregate of determinations that are constitutive for any and all determinancy. That the account of the logically necessary is not limited to the simply tautologous is clearly shown by the *Logic* itself, even in isolation from the Philosophies of Nature and Spirit. Yet regardless of the wealth of detail developed in Hegel's sciences, there is a prima facie plausibility to Schelling's claim that a system that cannot explain both why the world is precisely as it is, and why there is something rather than nothing, cannot complete philosophy in wisdom. This plausibility derives from the vague presupposition that wisdom, as absolute knowledge, would be a comprehensive knowledge of "what the case is." Hegel can claim to have attained absolute knowledge only by radically rejecting precisely this presupposition; this is the third aspect of his fundamental disagreement with Schelling.

The question of what an absolute knowing would be is often made more concrete—or at least more easily approachable—by its restatement as the question of what would be known by an infinite intellect, one not sharing our obvious perceptual, corporeal, and temporal limitations. The pre-Kantian standpoint of the understanding can, according to Hegel, imagine the infinitude of the absolute intellect only as a sort of quantitative all-inclusiveness. Hegel both illustrates and satirizes this view by quoting part of a funeral oration included in a contemporary novel, a work, according to Hegel, "of the deepest humor":

> "Neighbor Briese was speaking to me yesterday of the greatness of dear God's love, and it occurred to me that dear God would be able to call every sparrow, every goldfinch, every linnet, every mite, every gnat by name, as you do the people in the village: 'Greger Schmied, Peter Briesen, Hans Heifried'—just imagine dear God calling every gnat like that, when they look so much alike you'd swear they were all sisters and brothers; just imagine!"[3]

This view is, according to Hegel, grounded in the understanding's failure to distinguish among, and thus to evaluate properly, various sorts of infinities:

> Even the universal is infinite; the respect for the infinite that keeps the understanding from recognizing it in every universal is an absurd respect. The infinite is high and mighty, but the positing of its height and might in that countless horde of gnats, the positing of the infinitude of knowing in acquaintance with those numberless gnats, that is, with the individual gnats, such positing reveals not the incapacity of faith, reason, and spirit [to grasp infinitude], but rather the incapacity of the understanding to grasp the finite as nugatory, to grasp its being as of a sort that, as only such, has the value and significance only of non-being.
>
> Spirit is immortal, it is eternal; it is such precisely in that it is infinite, that it is not spatially finite, not these five feet of height, two feet of breadth and width of the body, not the now of time, its knowledge not a content in it of these innumerable gnats, and its will, its freedom not the infinite mass of resistances, nor of the ends and activities that are opposed by such resistances and hindrances. The infinitude of spirit is its being in itself, abstractly, its pure being in itself, and this is its thought, and this abstract thought is an actual, present infinitude, and its concrete being in itself is that this thinking is spirit (*TW*17: 478-79).

According to Hegel, it is in comprehensively thinking its own functional determinations—the pure concepts or categories—that any spirit, regardless of any sort of corporeal finitude, achieves absoluteness and thereby wisdom. In thinking those concepts and categories, we know the same truth that the infinite intellect would know—even if we cannot make as many correct judgments—and we know that our merely human limitations are nothing more than contingent aspects of what is, matters of fact that have "the value and significance only of non-being." The specifics of the world in which we as humans live are also, for the most part, such mere matters of fact—which, as such, are of no more philosophical importance than are mere matters of fancy (*L*2:247-48/SL:608)—and while, for example, progress in the physical sciences may continue to provide information about the factical realm in which we find ourselves, that information will increase only our capacity to make correct judgments, not our knowledge of the truth.

Hegel thus sees the irrationalities of the factical world as no threat to the wisdom attainable by the human sage. Nor is Hegel intimidated by Schelling's "final question," the puzzle: "Why is there anything at all? Why is there not nothing?" In fact, this question can arise only in an investigation that presupposes that we can have access only to relative grounds, and not to the absolute. Schelling's question can be asked sensibly only by a finite being seeking the cause of its existence as finite; the question makes sense only if the "something" about which it asks is a part, and not the whole. Schelling's God may be a ground that could, in a sense, explain the existence of the world, but it is not a ground that could, in the last instance, explain its own being. That there is, in the broadest sense, "something" rather than "nothing" is a fact that cannot have a reason; the reason would have to be grounded in a presupposed "something," but there can be no such transcendent "something" beyond the "something" that is the whole. Schelling takes the regress a step beyond man, and arbitrarily allows it to stop there; Hegel recognizes it as an infinite regress in which no stage will be adequate, thus as a regress that is avoided as soon as its structure is understood. Schelling's "final question" is one that can appear compelling only to man, not to God—and not, therefore, to the Hegelian sage.

Hegel's wisdom thus purports to be independent of all facticity. Hegel's disdain for aspects of the merely real that fall short of the rational has been aptly and dramatically expressed by Ernst Bloch:

> Hegel robustly attacks the supposedly unbridgeable gap between subject and object with the appetite of the animal that goes right up to the object and devours it. The thing in itself is grasped by the animal as what it is, as thing for us; it is grasped with the teeth. And if there remain bones that resist the tooth of the Concept, the proudly rational (*vernunftstolz*) Hegel discards them as worthless rather than worshiping them as impenetrable.[4]

THE REAL AND THE IDEAL

Schelling insists that Hegel cannot account for the contingent in the full wealth of its detail, and Hegel responds that he need not. Be that modality as it may, however, the question remains of whether Hegel can—or need—cope with the problem of nihilism. Although he is not concerned with the contingent as such, he is concerned, throughout the Philosophy of Spirit, with the plight of the finite spiritual being confronted with a factical—and thus contingent—reality. That there are many ways in which the individual spiritual entity may attempt to determine both itself and its world is a fact grounded in the Logic of the Concept. That nihilism is one attitude that may be adopted by the individual is a matter concretely considered in the subscience that has as its subject matter the comportment of the spiritual individual as active in a real world; that subscience is the Philosophy of Right.

The problem of nihilism is introduced by Hegel, non-scientifically, in the Preface to the *Philosophy of Right*. There, Hegel notes a recent natural-scientific tendency to relativism, that is, to the conviction that all value judgments are matters of opinion relative to individuals, times, and circumstances. This sort of relativism is presented as a theoretical nihilism; it is theoretical in that it grounds a way of thinking but—since individuals continue to judge acts as right or wrong—not a way of acting. The theory may be overcome, according to Hegel, only by the demonstration that right and wrong are determinations of thought that have specifiable contents (*PdR*:23-24/PoR:8-10). To the extent that determinations of value are necessary determinations of thought they are, furthermore, of interest to the philosopher—but only to that extent are they of interest to him. He is not concerned with changing what is wrong to make it more closely resemble what would be right, or with indicating how such change could or should be instigated. To the extent that the philosopher examines the factical at all, he does so only in order to recognize the traces of the rational, of the Idea, that are visible in the real order. For the philosopher to make practical suggestions would be for him to "interfere with things that do not concern him." (*PdR*:25/PoR:11)

Not only is it not the business of the philosopher to make concrete practical suggestions. The true philosopher also, according to Hegel, recognizes the senselessness of the attempt to construct an ideal state in which actual human beings would be imagined as attaining complete satisfaction. Thinkers who seek such ideals remain fixated at the *Logic's* penultimate stage, that of the Idea of the Good; they have not realized that the factical, precisely because it is factical, will never fully correspond to the rational. The Hegelian sage recognizes that in fact reason is "the rose in the cross of the present," and that while it must be and will be visible as the rose in the cross of every present, there can also never be a present free of the cross that finite subjects must bear (*PdR*:26/PoR:12). Recognition of the fact that the real—no matter how "monstrous," to use Schelling's term—can never be wholly devoid of rational elements (where there is no reason, there remains only the Parmenidean altogether-not), "rational insight" into that fact is itself the true sage's "reconciliation with actuality." The sage is thus not in conflict with the state—any state—as it exists; he is in conflict at most with inadequate accounts of the essence of the state, with bad theories. Actual approximations of rational truths are all—regardless of the precise degree of difference from the truth—contents that are, for reason, "neither warm nor cold," and thus "fit only to be spit out," not to be ingested (*PdR*:27/ PoR:12).

This description of the interest of the sage should make it clear that the standpoint of nihilism can arise in the Philosophy of Right itself not as a wrong that should be righted, but as a rationally defective viewpoint whose falsity must be revealed. That viewpoint arises in the dialectical development as the culmination of the second sphere of the science. The first sphere is devoted to Abstract Right. With the demonstration that the formal and objective demands of that Right remain external to the subject as subject—in that they attempt to govern acts alone, and not intentions—the move is made to the second sphere, that of Morality. Here the focus is on the subject's attempts at self-determination in accordance with what it takes to be right. The subject who fully thinks through the nature of Morality comes finally to recognize that he himself is the absolute source not only of his own determination, but of the "right" itself. At this point, the subject must make the choice between good and evil. The subject who takes itself to be absolute qua individual, and thus to be justified in acting in accordance with its contingent whims and fancies, is evil, and its reasoning is false; the truth is that the subject is absolute only qua rational, qua spiritual, and not simply qua individual (see *PdR*:§139Z).

The nihilistic position—which, most completely developed, appears as the "ironic" stance of an "absolute sophistry" (*PdR*:§140,A,Z)—thus remains fixated within the sphere of one-sided subjectivity. Hegel sees such fixation as the source of the greatest political errors of his time:

> Recently, the atomistic view of the *political* has become even more important than that of the physical. According to the former, it is the will of the *individuals* as such that is the principle of the state; what brings them together is the particularity of needs and inclinations; and the universal, the state itself, is the external relation of the contract(E:§98A).

This "syllogism" uniting individuals through their needs into the external and abstract universal of the political government is pre-

sented in the *Logic* itself as a defective analysis of the moments of
the political whole; it is used there to clarify the inadequacy of the
"syllogism of appearance" (*L*2:374/*SL*:723-24). In fact, according to Hegel, the spiritual unity of all rational individuals—their
identity with respect to essence, as absolute sources of determination sharing the same principles of determination—is ignored by
all who remain at subjective standpoints. With the recognition
that the account remains one-sided if the political whole is not
considered, the third sphere of the Philosophy of Right is entered.
Therein the contradiction between external Right and internal
Morality is overcome not through denial of either, but rather
through their reconciliation in the idea of the state.

The course of Hegel's argumentation need not be considered
here; important for present purposes are his conclusions. The first
of these is that the individual "comes to his right" not in acting
as an atomic unit, but in being "citizen of a good state"
(*PdR*:§153Z, §261A). The state is good to the extent that its
grounding notions of law and government correspond to the rational determinations of such things (see §272, §272A, §273Z).
Again, however, no state is perfectly good or bad. Not the latter,
for even "the worst state, whose reality is least correspondent to
the Concept, is still, insofar as it exists, the Idea; the individuals
obey a concept that is in power" (*L*2:409/*SL*:758). The state cannot be perfectly good because it "is not a work of art, it is in the
world and thus in the sphere of arbitrariness, of accident and error (*PdR*:§258Z)."

The unavoidable imperfection of the state prevents it from serv-
ing as the arena in which spirit may find its absolute satisfaction;
therefore, the speculative philosopher moves from the sphere of
Right, of Objective Spirit, to that of Absolute Spirit, wherein determination is not essentially limited by that which is determined.
For reasons suggested in the passage just quoted, spirit first attempts to attain absolute satisfaction through Art, through a determination of external material that is a self-expression rather
than a self-limitation. The Artistic attempt remains, however,
too closely bound to what is, which generally serves as the source
of its subject matter; it gives way to the Religious, and the latter,
finally, to the Philosophical.

The political realm is, for Hegel, one in which at best a limited rational satisfaction may be attained. Nevertheless, according to Hegel, in all but the very worst states it is rational for the individual to be a good citizen, for the political is one of the necessary modes of finite spiritual existence. If however the state is entirely corrupt, the philosopher will look only to himself, seeking inner satisfaction in Art, Religion, and Philosophy (*PdR*:§138, §138Z). Revolution is not a philosophical response, for the philosopher knows that true satisfaction is in any case to be attained only in the realm of Absolute, not in that of Objective Spirit.[5] The revolutionary is no more philosophically enlightened than is the petty critic who stupidly seeks only to prove that a given state is less than ideal:

> If the understanding turns with its "ought" to trivial, external, and transitory objects, institutions, conditions, and so forth, which may be of great relative importance for a certain time or in particular circles, then it may be right, and it may find much in such things that does not correspond to the universal and correct determinations; could there be anyone so lacking in cleverness as to be unable to see much in his environs that is not as it should be? But this cleverness errs in imagining that with such objects and their "oughts," it has a place of interest within the philosophical science. The latter has to do only with the Idea, which is not so impotent that it only ought to be, that it is not actually; philosophy thus treats an actuality of which those objects, institutions, conditions, and so forth are merely the superficial exterior (*E*:§6A).

The understanding, judging the real, may be right—its judgment may be correct—but it will not thereby attain the truth; it will exhibit at most its cleverness, for it has no wisdom to reveal.

The Hegelian sage does not nihilistically deny that there is a rationally determinable difference between right and wrong; he does not do so because such denial is irrational. At the same time, however, the sage is not particularly concerned with protecting society from the corrupting political influence of others' acceptance of such a nihilism, nor is he particularly concerned with using his knowledge of the difference between right and wrong to improve the lot of his fellow beings. Hegel never repudiates the claim, explicitly made as early as 1802, that an essential aspect of the truly philosophical attitude is stoical *ataraxia* (*TW*2:242), which is misrepresented by Schelling as an "unnatural struggle against an indomitable fate" (13:203).[6] In the words of the *Encyclopedia*: "In fact, philosophy is precisely this doctrine that frees man from an infinite number of finite ends and intentions, and makes him indifferent to them, so that it is all the same to him whether such things exist or not" (*E*:§88A).

METAPHYSICS AND ANTHROPOLOGY

Schelling insists that philosophy is a science of what is, that it must ground the convictions that give the life of the common man meaning, and that it can do so only by demonstrating that God grounds the world; Hegel argues that philosophy is a science of what cannot be otherwise, that its responsibility is to the demands of reason rather than to those of life, and that it satisfies those demands by demonstrating the ontological supremacy and sufficiency of first the Absolute Idea and then Absolute Spirit. Both Hegel and Schelling are generally known as philosophers, yet it might seem that they pursue such different ends that, finally, the wisdom they seek is the same in name only. The very source of their difference, however, reveals their essential relatedness. Both remain true to the Western metaphysical tradition: Hegel attempts to complete it with onto-theology, Schelling with theo-ontology.

Despite Schelling's aspirations and his claims, he was instrumental not in the completion of metaphysics, but rather in its abandonment. He convinced a rising generation of thinkers, first, that *anthropological* problems—existential and political ones—are vital to philosophy; second, that Hegel's failure to treat those problems reveals an essential limitation of his system—and one that cannot be avoided in any mere doctrine of categories; and third, unwittingly—through the manifest failure of positive philosophy to satisfy its own requirements—that these crucial anthropological problems are not to be solved through any rational metaphysical theology. In effect, then, Schelling convinced those who followed that the traditional bases of first philosophy—ontology and theology—are equally unsatisfactory as grounds for the study of the philosophical problems most important to human beings.

Despite Schelling's critique—and despite its historical effectiveness—Hegel's system is in principle defensible if it is interpreted ontologically. Schelling mediates the historical rejection of Hegelianism by claiming to reveal that anthropological problems are beyond the scope of Hegel's system; Hegel insists, however, that those problems are beneath him rather than beyond him. Hegel, indeed, could accept the relation of anthropology to ontology— and of Schelling's concerns to his own—that is suggested in Schelling's myth of Vishnu and Mahabala, first recounted above (p. 34). It bears retelling:

> The Hegelian Concept is the Indian god Vishnu in his third incarnation, in which he sets himself against Mahabala, the gigantic prince of darkness (and at the same time the spirit of ignorance), who has attained a position of supreme mastery in all three worlds. Vishnu appears to Mahabala first in the form of a small, dwarflike Brahmin, and asks him for only three feet of land (the three concepts Being, Nothingness, and Becoming). Scarcely has the giant granted this when the dwarf assumes a tremendous form. With his first step he takes in the earth, with his second heaven, and he is about to encompass hell with the third when Mahabala throws himself at Vishnu's feet and piously recognizes the power of the highest god. Vishnu then generously grants Mahabala mastery in the realm of darkness (only under his own supervision, of course) (10:144-45).

At a time, in the early 1800's, when Schelling had achieved a mastery of sorts in the German philosophical world, Hegel first appeared in the not particularly significant form of his disciple. Later, however, starting with Being, Nothingness, and Becoming, Hegel attempted to develop a system encompassing heaven (in the *Logic*) and earth (in the Philosophies of Nature and Spirit). Finally, Hegel, like Vishnu, did indeed leave the hell of factical existence to others. His objection to Schelling and to the other avatars of Mahabala who have followed him would be that they have not shown sufficient piety in accepting the responsibility of governing the human realm; all have attempted to put that hell in a context other than the Hegelian one and have thereby prevented themselves from developing philosophically adequate accounts of its problems.

The question raised by this heretical interpretation of Schelling's myth—the final question of this study—is that of whether Hegelian supervision for the realm of darkness is possible. Schelling convincingly shows that were Hegel's a real dialectic purporting to exhibit the absolute necessity of the development of what is in its historical entirety, then the Hegelian would be unable to account for man as free, and would thus be unable to address himself seriously to the most important anthropological questions. Hegel's dialectic is, however—if consequent—ideal rather than real, his system one of transcendental ontology rather than of transcendent theology. Hegel chooses not to treat the merely factical, the merely existent, because he accords it no greater value or importance than the contingently non-existent, that which might be but is not. It remains to be determined whether the choice is necessary—as it would be if treatment of the factical would contradict Hegel's principles—and, assuming that that necessity is denied, whether the choice is justified, whether it is ultimately rational for the sage to have no more than a bemused interest in what is.

Though Hegel does not directly treat the factical, it is to be stressed that the Hegelian doctrine grounding truth in the Absolute Idea does purport to provide rational criteria for the evaluation of at least the most important factical "objects, institutions, conditions, and so forth," for the determination of which are better and which are worse. Hegel's dialectical development of evaluative categories provides the ground, in principle, for a practical doctrine that avoids both the formalism of Kantian ethics, and the dogmatic reliance on intellectual intuition essential to the material ethics developed, as an alternative to Kant, by Max Scheler and Nicolai Hartmann.[7] Like the latter doctrine, the Hegelian teaching is articulated into specific, concrete values; like the former, it is a doctrine whose grounding in reason itself protects it, in principle, from charges of relativism.[8] Moreover, the doctrine of "political atomism"—central to one form of political nihilism—is one that is rejected within Hegel's system. The *Philosophy of Right* purports to establish that human beings have responsibilities to each other—in addition to (rather than instead of) responsibilities to themselves—and that these responsibilities are sufficiently ontologically determinable to reveal that anarchy and fascism are, as entirely one-sided, equally irrational as attempts to cope with the human situation. Hegel presents the idea of the state as a whole of conceptually interrelated parts that therein realize themselves as individuals; it is thus, according to Hegel, a *logical* error to see the state as nothing more than a makeshift contraption designed to allow fundamentally selfish, isolated individuals to coexist in some temporary semblance of harmony.

Hegel does not attempt to construct an ideal state. Even if such a construction were somehow possible—which he denies—it would not be possible within the framework of a pure transcendental ontology. Rather than presenting an ideal whole against which existent states could potentially be measured, then, Hegel provides conceptual analyses of the political structures that are dialectically derived as essential. Thus, for example, he claims to establish the necessity that crimes be punished, and while he insists that the determination of what punishment is appropriate for specific crimes is not a task for the sage—because contingent historical and cultural factors would be relevant, in every case, to the establishment of the just penal code—he does claim to reveal a fundamental categorial distinction between punishment and revenge, a distinction indicating the irrationality of grounding the former in the latter (*PdR:*§96Z,§103). While the Hegelian sage may not as such write codes of law, he may well present logical distinctions that would orient lawmakers with respect to what is right.

These considerations reveal that Hegel's system could, in principle, provide the first-philosophical ground for the development of an evaluative account of any state or society. The question becomes that of whether Hegel is justified in denying, albeit tacitly, that the development of such an account is a task for the philosopher. It is not clear how he could be. Granted that the philosopher is primarily concerned with what cannot be otherwise, it does not follow that he can have *no* philosophical concern with what is; granted that reason may be fully satisfied only in the realm of Absolute Spirit, it does not follow that, within the realm of Objective Spirit, a corrupt regime is to be ignored rather than transformed—especially by one who has, in principle, already exhausted the contents of the absolute realm.

The question may be put to Hegel in a slightly different form: if existential and political problems are not philosophical ones, what sort of problems are they? To the extent that they are to be solved, or approached, only through value judgments, and that value judgments are rationally grounded only through the Absolute Idea, they are clearly problems that cannot be adequately approached by those not thoroughly experienced in Hegelian dialectical analysis. It may be granted that it would be irrational for the sage to be led to despair by the imperfection and imperfectibility of the "conditions and institutions" that confront him, and that it would be irrational for him to subordinate philosophy to political activity. It may also be granted that it could be unwise for the sage to present his suggestions or demands for change aggressively: there have certainly been historical situations in which such preaching would have been both dangerous and counter-productive. At the same time, however, Hegel insists that even the sage should be a good citizen if he finds himself in a relatively just state, and that would certainly entail the attempt to preserve that justness.

Only a lengthy argument, if any, could establish the rational *necessity* for the sage to concern himself with the practical use of the results of his analyses. Independent of such an argument, however, the question may be raised of what the sage does after he has completed philosophy. The question is not considered within Hegel's system, but Hegel's own example provides a basis for judgment. It would appear that the sage, having fully appropriated the absolute categorial content, turns—in search of something like amusement rather than of a higher or further truth—from essence to existence. In his lectures, Hegel examined the factical developments of world history, art, religion, and philosophy, attempting to show that the dialectical structure of intelligibility is revealed in those realms: in each, there are visible dialectical relations in which later stages assimilate earlier ones, overcoming their defects. Still more important is the fact that Hegel asserts, in the Preface of the *Philosophy of Right*, that the philosopher is concerned with "grasping his time in thought," with determining how much of what is in his era is rational (*PdR:26/* PoR:11). The sage's analysis of his epoch would certainly have implications that could be practically applied, and, it could be argued, it would be irrational to entrust that application to agents who did not fully understand the analysis. That Hegel reasoned similarly is suggested by the fact that he himself wrote newspaper articles concerning contemporary political developments.

Hegel did concern himself with the analysis and evaluation of the factical world, but without clarifying the relation of that concern to the wisdom that completes philosophy. It might therefore appear that the activity of the sage, as a move beyond (or beneath) Absolute Spirit, is a merely human activity, that is, that the move from the ideal and necessary to the real but contingent suffers from at least some of the defects attributed by Schelling to the move from Logic to Nature. It appears to be the move of the human who, after all, must continue to do something, rather than of the avatar of spirit who, having recognized its own absoluteness, is fully satisfied. Even a move to the factical of this sort, however, would not threaten the system in the way that such a move from Logic to Nature would. Hegel's system is comprehensive with respect to the categorial, but it does not claim to be so with respect to the factical; thus, the account of the factical grounded in that of the categorial could never make the latter relative to the former. Moreover, the move to the factical would not be a dialectical one, nor would the account of the factical be dialectically structured. It could be so structured only if dialectical relations were real rather than ideal, only if they were relations of things rather than relations of ideas.

With the Hegelian move from ontology to existential anthropology, the dialectical thread would not continue, not because it would have been broken, but because its ends have already been joined at the completion of the categorial account. In claiming to have exhausted the dialectically structured categorial realm, Hegel claims to have completed philosophy. In fact, however, he has completed at best only first philosophy, his system represents at most the highest theoretical knowledge, that which grounds further inquiry. Grounding such inquiry is however quite different from completing it. In completing metaphysics, Hegel provides philosophical anthropology with the point from which it can begin.

The argument that the Hegelian need not simply ignore anthropological problems completes my defense of Hegel. The defense as a whole could be viewed as an answer to the question: Does it make sense to be a Hegelian? My arguments are intended to establish that it does make sense if, and only if, to be a Hegelian is to be a transcendental philosopher, to seek, as ground for all theoretical inquiry, a dialectically organized complex of categories discoverable in a genealogical investigation and determinable through speculative-logical reflection. To be a Hegelian, in this sense, is not dogmatically to accept or defend every word and sentence in the *Science of Logic* or in any other of the master's works, nor is it to insist that Hegel said everything of philosophical importance that can be said. It is, rather, to recognize the capacity of the categorial absolute for grounding investigation into all problems of philosophical interest and importance, and to be convinced that an adequate account of the categorial absolute may, in principle, be developed. To be a Hegelian in this sense is, further, to be convinced that the dialectical analysis of Right can lead to the determination of values that are neither culturally nor historically relative, and thus to the avoidance of nihilism.

To be a Hegelian, in this sense, is to accept the ontological solution to the problem of metaphysics, but one can accept that solution without then identifying metaphysics with philosophy.

Notes

NOTES TO INTRODUCTION

1. Peter K. Schneider's *Die Wissenschaftsbegründende Funktion der Transzendentalphilosophie* (Freiburg and Munich: 1965) is an excellent study revealing the incapacity of empirical science, and of any basically formal philosophy of science, to establish a ground for the truth claims of scientific judgments. Starting from considerations of the problems introduced by the observer effect in subatomic physics and of the conflicting claims of logicists, formalists, and intuitionists with respect to the foundations of mathematics, Schneider develops the argument that transcendental-philosophical grounding is the only sort that could satisfy all theoretical requirements.

2. *Schellings Abhandlung über das Wesen der menschlichen Freiheit* (Tübingen: Max Niemeyer, 1972), p. 78.

3. In supporting an "ontological" interpretation of Hegel, I am consciously following Klaus Hartmann, who has strongly influenced me. Unlike Hartmann, I do not term this reading "non-metaphysical"—although I did in my doctoral dissertation—because many with whom I have discussed Hegel have found the opposition of ontology to metaphysics needlessly confusing. Note 7 to Chapter Seven, below, indicates a substantive issue on which I differ from Hartmann.

   Hartmann's interpretation is presented most directly in "Hegel: A Non-Metaphysical View," in *Hegel. A Collection of Critical Essays*, ed. A. MacIntyre (Garden City, NY: Anchor, 1972), and in his Introduction to *Die ontologische Option*, ed. Klaus Hartmann (Berlin: Walter de Gruyter, 1976).

4. See Manfred Frank, *Der unendliche Mangel an Sein: Schellings Hegelkritik und die Anfänge der Marxschen Dialektik* (Frankfurt: Suhrkamp, 1975) and the references therein. Schelling's importance to post-Idealistic thinkers was first emphasized by Karl

161

Löwith in *From Hegel to Nietzsche* (New York: Doubleday, 1967).

5. See pp. 118-25 and 143-49, below.

6. I use the term "nihilism" broadly, to signify the conviction that there can be no knowledge of absolute values. Among the positions that are nihilistic in this sense are relativism, skepticism, and historicism. I am not interested, in this study, in the problem of nihilism itself, but rather in presenting one way in which the problem may potentially be avoided. Readers interested in the nihilistic consequences of the acceptance of mathematical-empirical science as the model for rational inquiry should see Leo Strauss's *Natural Right and History* (Chicago: University of Chicago Press, 1953), particularly the Introduction and Chapters I and II. On the nihilistic implications of contemporary analytic philosophy and of existentialism, see Stanley Rosen's *Nihilism* (New Haven: Yale University Press, 1969).

7. Throughout this study, "anthropology" refers to *philosophical* anthropology, the study of man (as opposed, *e.g.*, to ontology, the study of being, or theology, the study of God). This "anthropology" should not be confused with the modern social science.

8. My objections to the Schelling interpretations developed by Schulz, Horst Fuhrmans, and Harald Holz—the most important of the recent commentators—are given in the notes to Chapter Six, below.

9. I cover Schelling's entire career, emphasizing the coherence of his development, in *Schelling: An Introduction to the System of Freedom* (New Haven: Yale University Press, 1983).

NOTES TO CHAPTER ONE

1. F. W. J. Schelling, *Philosophie der Offenbarung* (Stuttgart and Augsburg: J. G. Cotta'scher Verlag, 1858; reprint ed., Darmstadt: Wissenschaftliche Buchgesellschaft, 1974), 1:60. For almost all references to Schelling's works, I have used the texts of the *Sämmtliche Werke*, originally published in 1856–61, as reprinted by the Wissenschaftliche Buchgesellschaft. Following standard procedure, I henceforth cite the *Werke* parenthetically, giving first volume number and then page. The present reference, so given, is 13:60. A key to all references to Schelling's works is provided in the Selected Bibliography, below.

Translations of German texts are my own.

2. G. W. F. Hegel, *Wissenschaft der Logik*, ed. G. Lasson, 3rd ed. (Hamburg: Felix Meiner, 1971), 1:7,36,46. I will refer to this work henceforth as the *Logic*, and cite it parenthetically as *L1* (first volume) or *L2*. SL designates the English translation, *Hegel's Science of Logic*, trans. A. V. Miller (New York: Humanities Press, 1969). The present reference is to SL:28,54,63.

3. F. W. J. Schelling, *Grundlegung der positiven Philosophie*, ed. with an introduction by Horst Fuhrmans (Torino: Bottega d'Erasmo, 1972), 223. Cited hereafter as *GPP*.

4. For Schelling's distinction between ideas and concepts, see pp. 49–50, below.

5. See pp. 105–18 below for a brief treatment of Schelling's development.

6. G. W. F. Hegel, *Enzyklopädie der philosophischen Wissenschaften im Grundrisse* (1830), ed. F. Nicolin and O. Pöggeler, 8th ed. (Hamburg: Felix Meiner, 1969). Cited parenthetically as *E*, followed by page numbers or, when possible, by section (§) numbers. "A" following a section number designates Hegel's explanatory note to the section.

   English translations: *The Logic of Hegel* (Part 1 of the *Encyclopedia*), trans. W. Wallace (Oxford: Clarendon, 1892); *Hegel's Philosophy of Nature* (Part 2 of the *Encyclopedia*), trans. A. V. Miller (Oxford: Clarendon, 1970); *Hegel's Philosophy of Mind* (Part 3 of the Encyclopedia), trans. W. Wallace and A. V. Miller (Oxford: Clarendon, 1971).

7. G. W. F. Hegel, *Phänomenologie des Geistes* (1807), ed. J. Hoffmeister, 6th ed. (Hamburg: Felix Meiner, 1952). English translation: *Phenomenology of Spirit*, trans. A. V. Miller (Oxford: Clarendon, 1977). Cited parenthetically as *PG* (German) and PS (English). The present reference is to *PG*:25/PS:15.

8. On the importance of the dialectical method to all of Hegel's sciences, see especially G. W. F. Hegel, *Grundlinien der Philosophie des Rechts*, in *Werke in zwanzig Bänden*, ed. E. Moldenhauer and K. M. Michel (Frankfurt: Suhrkamp, 1970), Vol. 7; §2, §2A. English translation: *Hegel's Philosophy of Right*, trans. T. M. Knox (London and New York: Oxford University Press, 1969). Cited henceforth as *PdR* (German) / PoR (English). "A" signifies *Anmerkung*, a Hegelian note to a section proper, and "Z" *Zusatz*, an addition made to Hegel's text by an editor, on the basis of Hegel's notes or of notes taken by students. On the status of the *Zusätze*, see *PdR*:527–29.

On the reliance of the *Phenomenology* on the form of the *Logic*, see *L*1:7/SL:28–9.

9. For a valuable study of the testing process, see R. Aschenberg, "Der Wahrheitsbegriff in Hegels *Phänomenologie des Geistes*," in *Ontologische Option*, ed. K. Hartmann, pp. 211–304. Other helpful treatments of the *Phenomenology* and its method are: Jean Hyppolite's detailed commentary, *Genesis and Structure of Hegel's Phenomenology of Spirit* (Evanston: Northwestern University Press, 1974); Pierre-Jean Labarrière's study of the form of the work, *Structures et mouvement dialectique dans la Phénoménologie de l'esprit de Hegel* (Paris: Aubier-Montaigne, 1968); Alexandre Kojève's fascinating and influential anthropological interpretation *Introduction to the Reading of Hegel* (New York: Basic Books, 1969); Chapters 6–9 of Stanley Rosen's *G. W. F. Hegel* (New Haven: Yale University Press, 1974); Chapters 2 and 3 of Hans-Georg Gadamer's *Hegel's Dialectic* (New Haven: Yale University Press, 1976); and Chapters 4 and 5 of J. N. Findlay's *Hegel: A Re-examination* (London: Allen and Unwin, 1958).

A very valuable work, one that deserves far more attention than it has received, is Johannes Heinrichs's *Die Logik der 'Phänomenologie des Geistes'* (Bonn: Bouvier, 1974). On Heinrichs, see note 10, below.

10. The problem of the difference in standpoint between the *Phenomenology* of 1807 and the later encyclopedic sciences has long been of central concern to Hegel scholars. It has, in my view, been solved by Johannes Heinrichs in *Die Logik der 'Phänomenologie des Geistes.'* Heinrichs argues convincingly that the 1807 version is not simply a naive variant of the later Philosophy of Spirit. According to Heinrichs, all of the encyclopedic sciences are explicitly presented from Hegel's scientific standpoint, and intended for readers already at that standpoint. For the *Phenomenology* of 1807, however, three standpoints are relevant: First, there is the standpoint of "natural consciousness," the stances of which are observed and described by the phenomenologist; the phenomenologist moves from stance to stance, but natural consciousness does not. Second, there is the standpoint of the phenomenologist, who, through observation of the attempts of natural consciousness, is led to the speculative standpoint. Third, there is the standpoint of the Hegelian scientist, who, from his absolute standpoint (from his complete knowledge of the contents of the *Phenomenology*), can aid the

phenomenologist in understanding the development. The *Pheno-menology*, unlike the Philosophy of Spirit, is written "for us" as philosophers seeking the truth, and not for the scientist, who knows the truth in general and is in the process of assimilating its specifics. The fact that "our" standpoint changes explains the description of the *Phenomenology* as the science of the experience of consciousness. The difference in expositional status between the two accounts—the encyclopedic and the purely phenomenological—in no way indicates a systematic defect.

Heinrichs introduces the three standpoints relevant to the 1807 work on p. 13; for his summary of the relation of the *Phenomenology* to the full system, see pp. 507–10.

11. On the non-scientific character of Hegel's prefaces and introductions, see *L*1:23–24, 29–30/*SL*:43–44, 54–55; *E*:§§18, 19A,20A,79. Werner Flach emphasizes the importance of these texts in "Zum 'Vorbegriff' der kleinen Logik Hegels," in *Der Idealismus und seine Gegenwart. Festschrift für Werner Marx zum 65.Geburtstag*, ed. U. Guzzoni, B. Rang, and L. Siep (Hamburg: Felix Meiner, 1976), pp. 133–47.

12. On the basis of Hegel's statement that the beginning must neither be nor appear arbitrary (*L*1:57/*SL*:72), H. F. Fulda has argued that the decision to think pure thought must be quite explicitly grounded: *Das Problem einer Einleitung in Hegels Wissenschaft der Logik* (Frankfurt: Klostermann, 1965), p. 44. It is however the beginning with Being that must be and appear necessary, given the decision to consider pure thought; the decision itself, taken in isolation from the *Phenomenology*, is arbitrary in a non-objectionable sense, as Hegel himself stresses in the passage quoted above.

   Fulda's is the most detailed available treatment of the controversy concerning the meaning of Hegel's "presuppositionlessness." Fulda considers not only the problem itself, but also various solutions suggested by others.

13. See Immanuel Kant, *Kritik der reinen Vernunft*, ed. Raymund Schmidt (Hamburg: Felix Meiner, 1926; reprint ed. 1971). English translation by Norman Kemp Smith, *Critique of Pure Reason* (New York: St. Martin's Press, 1965). I cite this work with page numbers from the 1871 (A) and 1878 (B) editions (which are indicated in Smith's translation). On the "Copernican revolution" in philosophy, see Bxvi–xix.

14. The translation process is further clarified in the section of the *Vor-

lesungen über die Philosophie der Religion entitled "Die Dialektik der Vorstellung," and in the seventh of the *Vorlesungen über die Beweise vom Dasein Gottes.* Both are contained in the seventeenth volume of the Suhrkamp *Werke in zwanzig Bänden;* since that edition is known as the *Theorie-Werkausgabe,* I indicate its volumes with "*TW*". The present references are *TW*17:152-56,391-99.

15. I use both "sublation" and "overcoming" to render Hegel's *Aufhebung.* A contradiction is sublated (*aufgehoben*) when its elements have been redetermined in such a way that a distinction between them remains while the contradiction—which would make the elements indeterminate—is avoided. See pp. 36–37 below, and *L*1:93-95/*SL*:106-108.

NOTES TO CHAPTER TWO

1. Schelling's dialectic is further considered below, pp. 107–08.
2. That Hegel can have no method independent of the movement of the pure thoughts themselves is at times recognized by Dieter Henrich, e.g., in "Anfang und Methode der Logik" (in *Hegel im Kontext,* Frankfurt: Suhrkamp, 1967), p. 93 ("Ergebnis Nr. 3"), in "Hegels Logik der Reflexion" (*Hegel im Kontext*), p. 102, and especially in "Hegels Grundoperation" (in *Der Idealismus und seine Gegenwart,* ed. Guzzoni et al.), pp. 212, 225, 226. Yet Henrich also insists that while at times—most clearly in the Logic of Being—the "semiotic process" in which the thoughts organize themselves must be autonomous ("Grundoperation," p. 226), Hegel must nevertheless have a determinable "deductive process," structured by a *formal* "fundamental operation," if his *Logic* is to be defensible against claims that its development is arbitrary ("Grundoperation," pp. 212,213,227).

   Since Henrich has not yet—to my knowledge—provided a full account either of the relation of the semiotic and deductive processes ("Grundoperation," p. 227) or of the fundamental operation of the deductive process itself (p. 228), it is difficult to criticize his interpretation. It is clear, however, that the unification of the processes will require very careful anayses if contradictions are to be avoided. For example: whereas the semiotic process seems to require that there be no independently describable "motor" for the dialectic, Henrich seems at times to view the "fundamental operation" as a functioning motor in the Logic of Being ("Anfang und Methode," p. 93), and as fully described as such in the Logic of Reflection ("Grundoperation," p. 223). The Logic of Reflection is seen by Henrich as the center of the *Logic*, dividing the book into two halves (p. 223), yet he has difficulty describing the status of either of these halves. He is not sure that a Logic of Being—which cannot, in principle, rely on the fundamental operation—is even possible (p. 226), and though he discusses Being and Nothingness in some detail, he does not even suggest how the move to Becoming might be possible "Anfang und Methode"). The inadequacy of Henrich's interpretation of the Logic of the Concept is indicated by the fact that he regularly presents the Concept as having only two "structural aspects" ("Hegels Logik der Reflexion," pp. 153–54, "Grundoperation," p. 224); for Hegel, it must have three.

Henrich's discussions of the "fundamental operation" itself, the operation of "autonomous negation," are vitiated to a considerable extent in that they are grounded in the misconception that Hegel conceived of formal-logical negation as propositional rather than as conceptual ("Grundoperation," p. 214–15, 217–18; see also "Formen der Negation in Hegels Logik," in *Hegel-Jahrbuch* 1974, pp. 247, 250, 252, 254). On this point, see also note 4 below. For further criticism of Henrich's treatment of Hegelian negation, see Werner Flach's "Zum 'Vorbegriff' der kleinen Logik Hegels," p. 140 and note 54.

3. Klaus Harlander, in *Absolute Subjektivität und kategoriale Anschauung* (Meisenheim am Glan: Verlag Anton Hain, 1969), develops a general understanding of the *Logic* close to my own (see his "three global theses," p. 50), but his project is misdirected through its faulty grasp of the function of the method. Harlander's central question concerns the ability of the method to produce the categorial content; as is indicated above, however, there can be no externally applicable method or tool that would determine which category comes where. Rather, the development must be experiential, it must be linear, and its general features may be formulated only retrospectively, at the point of its completion. Unquestionably, no moment is fully understood at the point where it arises in the linear development. Its placement in the architectonic of the whole is also necessary. Nonetheless, if the development is to proceed without question-begging, the linear development must not depend upon anticipation of the architectonic (*pace* Klaus Hartmann), any more

than on direct reference to the empirical contents of consciousness.

For a more complete evaluation of Harlander's book, see the review by Klaus Hartmann, in *Hegel-Studien* 7 (1972).

4. Thomas Seebohm, "The Grammar of Hegel's Dialectic," *Hegel-Studien* 11 (1976): 149–80, and "Das Widerspruchsprinzip in der Kantischen Logik und der Hegelschen Dialektik," *Akten des 4. Internationalen Kant-Kongresses* (Berlin: Walter de Gruyter, 1974), Teil II.2: 862–74. The difference between Hegel and the current logician, as revealed by Seebohm, is perhaps clearest in the case of the term "contradiction": within a propositional logic, given two propositions p and − p, one must be true and the other false. In the context of a Kantian logic of concepts, however, if two judgments "S is P" and "S is − P" (where P and − P are intensional correlates) are both asserted or derived, then *neither* is true, because the subject S is not determined at all if contradictory predicates are attributed to it. Since the Hegelian significations of negation and contradiction are derived within the Logic of Essence, they should cause difficulty only to those who unreflectively assume that they are used in what have come—relatively recently—to be their "ordinary" significations. At the same time, since the tendency to try to understand the terms by associating them to ordinary language (even the ordinary language of the logician) is so natural, Seebohm's detailed, formalized account of how the operators are used in Kant's logic can be extremely helpful to those who would understand Hegel.

5. *L*2:497–98/*SL*:836-37; see also *L*2:253/*SL*:612–13 on the deficiency of counting with respect to conceptual determinations. The limitations of numerical forms are revealed as early as the Logic of Being: it is the intent of the counting subject, and not the counted items themselves, that determines in any given case "how many" items there are.

6. The moment of immediacy necessary to awareness of categories has been stressed by the neo-Kantian Heinrich Rickert, most directly in *Das Eine, die Einheit und die Eins* (2nd ed. Tübingen: Mohr, 1924). According to Rickert, the speculative logician's attempt to give an account of the "pure logical object" is dependent on the alogical—thus, intuitive—visibility of that object as a whole. The account must be of the moments or elements of the object, but these may be presented in any order, since all are equally clearly visible from the beginning (pp. 20–24; see also p. 87). Pure logic must thus be, in Rickert's terms, "heterothetic" rather than merely thetic

or antithetic: the transcendental logician must posit the alogical if he is even to begin to think the logical.

The Hegelian would object, first, that Rickert illicitly narrows the speculative-logical enterprise by focusing on the pure logical *object*. Second, the Hegelian may admit that "mere negation" is not sufficient as the motor of a dialectic (Rickert, p. 21). In the terms of Hegel's Logic of Essence, every positing is necessarily a pre-positing, or pre-supposing, of elements necessary for the full determination of what is posited. In the Hegelian view, then, Rickert's "pure logical object" is far too simple: in fact, the Absolute Idea in its entirety is "pre-supposed" by any and all thought. Of course, since the Idea is neither thing nor thinglike, it cannot be "seen"—intellectually intuited—at the outset as a whole. Rather, it is brought into focus only through dialectical-logical determination.

A lengthy "Hegelian" response to Rickert is presented by Richard Kroner, in "Anschauen und Denken. Kritische Bemerkungen zu Rickerts Heterothetischem Denkprinzip" (*Logos* XIII, 1924/5): 90-127. Kroner rightly stresses that Hegel does not deny that speculative-logical thought is intuitive—any awareness at all requires the moment of immediacy (see pp. 91, 122-27)—but he does not clearly reveal the nature of Hegel's dialectic. He thus seems to leave himself, and Hegel, open to the heterothetic critique presented by Werner Flach in *Negation und Andersheit* (Munich: Ernst Reinhardt Verlag, 1959). Flach relies, however, on an inadequate understanding of Hegel, viewing his dialectic as a formal movement through thesis, antithesis, and synthesis (p. 13), and accepting as fundamental to Hegel the claim that all is contradictory (p. 39; see also pp. 61-63). While Flach is sensitive to the fundamental problems of speculative logic, he does not, in *Negation und Andersheit*, provide an adequate account of the Hegelian approach to those problems. He is much more sensitive to Hegel's subtleties in "Zum 'Vorbegriff' der kleinen Logik Hegels," where he stresses Hegel's insistence that pure logical thought requires intuition as well as discursion, indirectly indicating thereby the inaccuracy of Rickert's assumption that Hegel's thought purports to depend exclusively on the mediate relation of logical negation.

7. Dominique Dubarle, "Dialectique hégélienne et formalisation," in Dominique Dubarle and André Doz, *Logique et dialectique* (Paris: Librairie Larousse, 1972), pp. 1-193. The Seebohm references are given in Note 4, above.

8. Two recent forms of the claim that there are many possible speculative logics should be noted. One is that of Thomas Seebohm. Having argued that Hegel's notions of negation and contradiction are
essentially the same as Kant's, Seebohm begins to develop a critique
of Hegel. He asserts first that the consideration of formal logic in
Hegel's Logic of the Concept relies on Kant ("Grammar of Hegel's
Dialectic," p. 151). But he does not consider the section of the *Logic*
entitled "Determinations of Reflection," where Hegel purports to
derive the notions as necessary. This omission lends credence to Seebohm's suggestion that Hegel externally appropriates a formal logic, and that *other* speculative logics could be developed from other
formal logics (p. 180). The criticism would be telling if Seebohm
had established that Hegel's development indeed relies on an externally presupposed formal logic. For that, he would have had to
show that the experiential development of the *Logic* is incoherent
—which he does not attempt to do—or that the terms ultimately
used by Hegel metatheoretically are arbitrarily introduced. On the
latter point, he does not, as indicated above, even consider the section in which the terms are introduced into the *Logic*. Seebohm
does not directly argue either that thought cannot begin to think itself by thinking pure Being, or that it can begin to think itself by
thinking something else. His critique is thus ineffective against the
mode of development I have attributed to Hegel's *Logic*. The value
of his logical analyses—indicated in Note 4, Chapter 3, above—is
however independent of the success or failure of the critique.

Hans Wagner, in *Philosophie und Reflexion* (Munich and Basel:
Ernst Reinhard Verlag, 2nd ed. 1959), also denies that there can be
but one speculative logic. Wagner is in general agreement with Hegel in arguing that the "absolute predicate"—the predicate capable
of adequately determining the absolute—is necessary as the ground
of all other knowledge. According to Wagner, this predicate is con-
stituted by pairs of determinations including subject–object, thinking–being, ground–consequence, content–form, and unity–multiplicity (p. 135). The individual thoughts or moments are determined through (1) their relations of opposition to their comple-
ments, and (2) specifiable and determinate relations to all other
pairs of correlates. Further, the speculative explanation of the
absolute predicate can start with any of the pairs: "Each choice has
its advantages and disadvantages, and Schelling under- rather than
overestimated in saying he believed that the explanation of the
fundamental alternatives 'could easily be made in ten different

ways' " (p. 136). Yet, as I have indicated, if the different accounts determine the fundamental concepts differently, then there are various "absolute predicates," and Wagner lacks the ground he needs. If, however, Wagner means that the same account results from any start—in that there can be only one developed whole—then he is not truly in opposition to Hegel. It might be added that Wagner would have at least some difficulty in identifying the fundamental concepts—a difficulty avoided, at least in principle, by Hegel's dialectical development of the Absolute Idea.

NOTES TO CHAPTER THREE

1. See, e.g., *E*:§85, §86, §86A, §87A, §112A, §115A, §115A, §181A, §213A, §384A.
2. See, e.g., *PG*:24/*PS*:14, *PG*:31/*PS*:20, *PG*:33/*PS*:22, *L*1:23/*SL*:43, *L*1:30/*SL*:50, *L*1:31/*SL*:56-57; *E*:§28A, §31A, §33A, §41, §48A, §85, §162A, §246A.
3. Immanuel Kant, "Welches sind die wirklichen Fortschritte, die die Metaphysik seit Leibnizens und Wolffs Zeiten in Deutschland gemacht hat?" in *Werke in Zehn Bänden*, ed. W. Weischedel (Darmstadt: Wissenschaftliche Buchgesellschaft, 4th ed. 1959), pp. 590-91 (pp. 10-12 of the *Erste Handschrift*).
4. The German Idealists generally stress that "synthesis" can only follow "thesis" and "antithesis," but the point is basically a logical one deriving from the meanings of the terms themselves. This general claim is taken far too concretely by those who see in Hegelian dialectic a formal movement from thesis through antithesis to synthesis.
5. For the part played by the "sensibly given manifold" in Kant's doctrine of perception, see the fascinating and important works by Gerold Prauss: *Erscheinung bei Kant. Ein Problem der "Kritik der reinen Vernunft"* (Berlin: Walter de Gruyter and Co., 1971), *Kant und das Problem der Dinge an sich* (Bonn: Bouvier, 2nd ed. 1977), and *Einführung in die Erkenntnistheorie* (Darmstadt: Wissenschaftliche Buchgesellschaft, 1980). Unfortunately, Prauss, like Kant, is concerned chiefly with grounding empirical knowledge; he does not directly consider the problems of grounding transcendental knowledge.

6. On truth and correctness, see, e.g., *L*2:232-34/SL:592-93, *L*2:246-48/SL:607-608, *L*2:278/SL:636, *L*2:355/SL:706, *L*2:389/SL:737, *L*2:408-409/SL:757-58; *E*:§172A, §173A, §193A, §231A, §231A, §548A. See also Klaus Hartmann, Introduction to *Ontologische Option*, p. 18. On truth and correctness in the *Phenomenology*, see R. Aschenberg, "Der Wahrheitsbegriff," esp. pp. 302-305.

   Hegel applies his distinction also in his aesthetics: merely representational works of art can be at best correct, they cannot be true (see *TW*13:67, esp. 105-106).

   For Hegel's critique of previous ontologies, see esp. *E*:§33, §33A.

NOTE TO CHAPTER FOUR

1. Schelling's phrasing here emphasizes his conviction that only a theological doctrine can give life meaning. Earlier, for example in "Philosophical Letters Concerning Dogmatism and Criticism" (1795), he had recognized that the "struggle against an indomitable fate"—now termed "unnatural"—grounds human dignity and the aesthetic experience. In both the *System* of 1800 and in his lectures on the Philosophy of Art, he had also seen artistic activity as a means of fulfillment even for human beings confronted by an intrinsically meaningless universe.

NOTES TO CHAPTER FIVE

1. Lucian's phrasing identifies him as a Fichtean: in 1794, Fichte criticized Spinoza for taking the unjustified step "beyond the pure consciousness that is given in grounded consciousness," *Grundlage der gesammten Wissenschaftslehre*, in *Sämmtliche Werke*, ed. I. H. Fichte, vol. 1: *Zur theoretischen Philosophie 1* (Berlin, Veit and Co., 1845; reprint ed. Berlin: Walter de Gruyter, 1971): p. 101. Schelling often cites this phrase when criticizing Fichte; see, e.g., 4:353-55.

2. I term "scientific" those works presenting the system of identity in the Spinozist geometrical-deductive form, that which, according to the Schelling of 1801, allows "the greatest concision of exhibition and the most determinate evaluation of the evidence used in proofs" (4:113). These works are the *Exhibition*, the *Further Exhibitions*,

and the 1804 *System*. The dialogic works are *Bruno* (1802), "Philosophy and Religion" (1804), and *Of Human Freedom* (1809). Although only the first of these is presented as a discussion among individuals, "Philosophy and Religion" is presented as its sequel (6:13), and the *Freedom* essay is said to develop "conversationally," to be a dialogue in essence if not in superficial form (7:410n). In 1804, Schelling asserts that the dialogue is the form best suited to philosophy (6:13). On the distinction between—and relative importance of—the scientific and the dialogic works, see my book *Schelling*, chapters 3 and 4.

3. Marcel Proust, *The Guermantes Way*, trans. C. K. Scott Moncrieff (New York: Vintage/Random, 1970), p. 60.

4. See my *Schelling*, chapter 3, for an analysis.

5. Harald Holz argues that Schelling does rely on a form of the ontological proof, in *Spekulation und Faktizität. Zum Freiheitsbegriff des mittleren und späten Schelling* (Bonn: Bouvier, 1970), pp. 318, 321-22, 336-37, 366. Yet Holz admits that Schelling never thematizes "his" form of the argument, and sees the omission as a serious flaw in Schelling's account (p. 352). Holz also recognizes Schelling's claim that God's existence is provable only through experience, but then seems to accept the "experience of pure thought"—which teaches us, for example, that contradictories cannot be thought together (11:326)—as the relevant form of experience (Holz: 321–22, 322n). Yet, according to Schelling, that pure intellectual experience provides information only concerning what is possible, not what is actual (11:326), and thus cannot establish the actuality of God.

There are further difficulties with Holz's interpretation. Having taken God's existence to be proved independently of the world, Holz sees Schelling's system as bifurcated into a theology and a "philosophy," the latter treating the world and man (e.g., pp. 447, 462, 481, 486). He then criticizes Schelling for failing to thoroughly thematize God as such (p. 445), and he sees the link between the two parts of the system as problematic (p. 462). He further takes the specifics of the "fact of the world" to be relevant only to proving that man is grounded in his own fall (pp. 460, 462).

In my interpretation, Schelling is guilty neither of a systematic bifurcation nor of an only vaguely acknowledged reliance on the ontological proof. Schelling himself insists that the proof of God's existence is not merely a first part of his system: positive philosophy *as a whole* is intended to be a *progressive* proof of the existence of God (13:131, 248), and not an ontological one. One indication that it is not the latter is that it can never be completed (13:131). The problems seen as central by Holz derive not so much from his analyses of Schelling's works as from his attempts to reveal a purported fundamental reliance of Schelling on the Christian patristic tradition. His eagerness to establish his thesis concerning this influence makes him prone, it seems to me, to identify as the crucial Schellingian problems those that were most important to the patristic tradition.

6. Walter Schulz fails to recognize the crucial function of this empiricism in his extremely influential book, *Die Vollendung des deutschen Idealismus in der Spätphilosophie Schellings* (2nd. ed. Pfullingen: Neske, 1975). Schulz takes the late Schelling to believe that the real can be simply derived from the absolute; he takes the constructibility of the world—as confirmed by the correspondence of construct and reality in finite cases—to prove that the absolute is God (p.76; cf. p. 82). This would be Schelling's only option if Schulz were correct in asserting that "the possibility of experience of God must be excluded" because God is not a thing (p. 325). Schulz ignores Schelling's insistence that "empiricism . . . by no means excludes all knowledge of the supersensible (13:113)."

    Jürgen Habermas, in "Das Absolute in die Geschichte. Von der Zwiespalt in Schellings Denken" (unpublished inaugural dissertation, University of Bonn, 1954), also fails to recognize the importance of experience to positive philosophy, and consequently concludes that Schelling's appropriation of Kant's doctrine of the Ideal is "inconsequent," and that Schelling's negative and positive philosophies are incompatible (see pp. 208–12).

7. In the broadest sense, "negative" philosophy is the work of pure reason, in isolation from the experience of anything heterogenous to thought, while "positive" philosophy must be, or rely on, some form of sensible empiricism. The relevant senses are clarified by Schelling in various contexts; see e.g. 13:68, 76, 92–94, 130, 151–53, 158, 248n; 10:17–18, 109.

8. See p. 131, below.

9. Schelling often asserts that there must be various accounts (see, e.g., 11:299, 13:113, 248, 248n;; 14:344–45). He asserts that the situations in mathematics and philosophy are similar. To think speculatively is to consider various possible ways in which a given scientific end may be reached, just as to think mathematically is to consider

various possible proofs for a given theorem; there is often concern with the discovery of simpler proofs for theorems that have already been conclusively established (14:344–45). In mathematics, of course, there are clear rules of procedure, and clear tests for the adequacy of proofs. Since Schelling's speculative philosopher can rely on neither, the multiplicity of accounts can lead to the impression that Schelling simply presupposes that which is to be proved—the absolute as structured through the powers—and attempts, after the fact, to make his presupposition appear justified. The powers caused Schelling similar difficulties and led him to offer a comparable variety of accounts during the time in which he was developing the system of identity; see my *Schelling*, chapter 3.

10. It is thus clear that God is in no way now considered to be dependent on the *finite* world-process for his own self-knowledge, as the younger Schelling took him to be (compare 7:433 with 13:292). In that the later Schelling explicitly denies any dependence of God on the world (12:109, esp. *GPP*:469), Fuhrmans' thesis that Schelling continues to the end of his career to attempt to develop an explicative theology is highly questionable; see Horst Fuhrmans, *Schellings Philosophie der Weltalter* (Düsseldorf: Schwann, 1954), p. 447. At the same time, it is not clear that Schelling succeeds in keeping God free from the world: the ideal creation is necessary for divine self-knowledge, and it would appear that that creation ends only with the production of a humanity whose fall is foreseen by God.

11. It is Fuhrmans's underemphasis of this question that allows him (1) to assert that "positive philosophy" does not add anything fundamental to *Ages of the World (Schellings Weltalter*, p. 308; Introduction to GPP, *GPP*:14), (2) to imply that there could be other "parts" to positive philosophy besides the Philosophies of Mythology and Revelation (*GPP*:49); and (3) to insist that Schelling is concerned primarily with God rather than with the world (*Schellings Weltalter*, pp. 245, 447, 458).

   On the third point, Schulz and Fuhrmans are in peculiar agreement; both seem convinced that Schelling is primarily concerned with the absolute rather than with what follows from it. They differ fundamentally in characterizing the absolute, respectively, as reason and as God. But because of their placement of the system's focal point, both are unable to show why the later Schelling is so concerned with myth and religion.

12. On the resistance of the first principle as the source of irrationality see the *Freedom* essay, and my analysis of it in chapter 4 of *Schelling*.
13. Whereas Schulz does not grasp the importance of the second step, the positive one (see note 6, above), Fuhrmans misses that of the first. He takes dialectical derivations to fall completely in the realm of the negative; since God is free, Fuhrmans reasons, his acts cannot be derived, they must rather be examined as facts (*GPP*:20). For Schelling, however, analysis of the "fact of the world" is theologically fruitful only because the positive philosopher has determined, in advance, what he is looking for.
14. See, e.g., 1:157.
15. Sören Kierkegaard, letter of 27 February 1842 to Peter Christian Kierkegaard, included in F. W. J. Schelling, *Philosophie der Offenbarung 1841/2*, ed. with an introduction by Manfred Frank (Frankfurt: Suhrkamp, 1977), p. 456. By way of contrast: on 22 November 1841, after Schelling's second lecture in Berlin, Kierkegaard wrote in his journal that his joy was "indescribable," that he had "set all his hopes on Schelling" (pp. 452–53).
16. *Schelling*, esp. the excursus on Hegel's *Phenomenology*, pp. 104–106.
17. Many of Schelling's reflections on freedom and time, especially, are both fascinating and important. See Martin Heidegger, *Schellings Abhandlung über das Wesen der menschlichen Freiheit* (Tübingen: Niemeyer, 1972), and Wolfgang Wieland, *Schellings Lehre über die Zeit. Grundlage und Voraussetzungen der Weltalterphilosophie* (Heidelberg: Carl Winter-Universitätsverlag, 1956).

NOTES TO CHAPTER SIX

1. Fichte, *Sämmtliche Werke*, vol. 1, p. 176n.
2. For Hegel, such tautologous identities are in fact contradictions. The predicate in any judgment functions only insofar as it determines the subject; if the predicate merely repeats the term identifying the subject, there is no determination, so the judgmental form—or the copula—is contradicted. The point is made most clearly in the *Logic* on L2:30/SL:415; its importance was clear to Hegel as early as 1803 (see TW2:466). Such judgments are contradictory only in the logic of concepts, not in that of propositions (see Note 4 to Chapter 3, above).

3. Hegel quotes Theodor Gottlieb von Hippel, *Lebensläufe nach aufsteigender Linie* (3 Bde., Berlin: 1778/81).
4. Ernst Bloch, *Subjekt–Objekt. Erläuterungen zu Hegel*, expanded ed. (Frankfurt: Suhrkamp, 1962), p. 41.
5. This is not to say that revolution cannot be beneficial. For an analysis of Hegel's evaluation of revolution, see Joachim Ritter, "Hegel und die Französische Revolution," reprinted in *Metaphysik und Politik* (Frankfurt: Shurkamp, 1977), pp. 183-255. Ritter reveals the inadequacy of the view—popularized by Haym in 1857, and thereafter extremely influential—that Hegel became a complete opponent of revolution, and a reactionary apologist for the Prussian state (pp. 183–88).
6. See Note 1 to Chapter 5, above.
7. See Nicolai Hartmann, *Ethik* (Berlin and Leipzig: Walter de Gruyter, 1926), e.g. p. 56.
8. In insisting on the absolute validity of Hegel's *Logic*, I am in conscious opposition to Klaus Hartmann. Hartmann takes Hegel's doctrine to be "historical" in the sense that its validity for all times is not even claimed, much less proved ("Non-Metaphysical View," p. 122, *Ontologische Option* Introduction, pp. 6, 28). If this were the case, Hegel's teachings would be of negligible practical importance; Hegel would be unable to confront the problems of nihilism.

To accept the ahistorical validity of speculative logic is not necessarily to accept a fixed grid of categories: more important than comprehensiveness is circularity. Hegel must show that the conceptual relations present in the Logics of Being and of Essence are inadequate, and that that of the Logic of the Concept is comprehensive, but not all accounts revealing these truths need contain precisely the same categories. (This explains the differences between the *Science of Logic* and the shorter *Logic* included in the *Encyclopedia*.) The refutation of nihilism requires demonstration of the inadequacy of all practical views in nihilism's logical sphere.

Selected Bibliography

Aschenberg, Reinhardt. "Der Wahrheitsbegriff in Hegels *Phänomenologie des Geistes.*" In *Die ontologische Option*: 211–304. Edited by Klaus Hartmann. Berlin: Walter de Gruyter, 1976.

Bloch, Ernst. *Subjekt–Objekt. Erläuterungen zu Hegel*, expanded edition. Frankfurt: Suhrkamp, 1962.

Brinkmann, Klaus, "Schellings Hegel-Kritik." In *Die ontologische Option*. Edited by Klaus Hartmann. Berlin: Walter de Gruyter, 1976.

Dekker, Gerbrand. *Die Rückwendung zum Mythos. Schellings letzte Wandlung.* Munich and Berlin: R. Oldenbourg, 1930.

Dubarle, Dominique, and André Doz. *Logique et dialectique.* Paris: Librairie Larousse, 1972.

Fackenheim, Emil L. "Schellings Begriff der positiven Philosophie." *Zeitschrift für philosophische Forschung* VIII/3 (1954): 321–35.

Fichte, Johann Gottlieb. *Sämmtliche Werke.* Edited by Immanuel Hermann Fichte. Vol. 1: *Zur theoretischen Philosophie 1.* Berlin: Veit and Co., 1971.

Findlay, J. N. *Hegel: A Re-examination.* London: Allen and Unwin, 1958.

Flach, Werner. *Negation und Andersheit.* Munich: Ernst Reinhardt Verlag, 1959.

_____. "Zum 'Vorbegriff' der kleinen Logik Hegels." In *Der Idealismus und seine Gegenwart. Festschrift für Werner Marx zum 65. Geburtstag*: 133–147. Edited by U. Guzzoni, B. Rang, and L. Siep. Hamburg: Felix Meiner, 1976.

Frank, Manfred, *Der unendliche Mangel an Sein: Schellings Hegelkritik und die Anfänge der Marxschen Dialektik.* Frankfurt: Suhrkamp, 1975.

_____, and Kurz, G., eds. *Materialien zu Schellings Philosophischen Anfängen.* Frankfurt: Suhrkamp, 1975.

Fuhrmans, Horst. Foreword and Introduction to *Grundlegung der positiven Philosophie*, by F. W. J. Schelling. Torino: Bottega d'Erasmo, 1972.

_____. *Schellings Philosophie der Weltalter.* Düsseldorf: Schwann, 1954.

Fulda, Hans-Friedrich. *Das Problem einer Einleitung in Hegels Wissenschaft der Logik.* Frankfurt: Klostermann, 1965.

Gadamer, Hans-Georg. *Hegel's Dialectic.* New Haven: Yale University Press, 1976.

Habermas, Jürgen. "Das Absolute und die Geschichte. Von der Zwiespalt in Schellings Denken." Inaugural dissertation, University of Bonn, 1954.

Harlander, Klaus. *Absolute Subjektivität und kategoriale Anschauung. Eine Untersuchung der Systemstruktur bei Hegel.* Meisenheim am Glan: Verlag Anton Hain, 1969.

Hartmann, Klaus. "Hegel: A Non-Metaphysical View." In *Hegel. A Collection of Critical Essays,* pp. 101–24. Edited by A. MacIntyre. Garden City,N.Y.: Anchor, 1972.

_____. Introduction to *Die ontologische Option,* edited by Klaus Hartmann. Berlin: Walter de Gruyter, 1976.

_____. *Die Marxsche Theorie.* Berlin: Walter de Gruyter, 1970.

_____. Review of *Absolute Subjektiviät und kategoriale Anschauung,* by Klaus Harlander. *Hegel-Studien* 7 (1972).

Hartmann, Nicolai. *Die Philosophie des deutschen Idealismus.* 2nd ed. Berlin: Walter de Gruyter, 1960.

_____. *Ethik.* Berlin and Leipzig: Walter de Gruyter, 1926.

Hegel, Georg Wilhelm Friedrich. *Enzyklopädie der philosophischen Wissenschaften im Grundrisse (1830).* Edited by F. Nicolin and O. Pöggeler. 8th ed. Hamburg: Felix Meiner, 1969. Cited in the text as *E.* English translations: *The Logic of Hegel* (*E*, Pt. 1). Translated by W. Wallace. Oxford: Clarendon, 1892. *Hegel's Philosophy of Nature* (*E*, Pt. 2). Translated by A. V. Miller. Oxford: Clarendon, 1970. *Hegel's Philosophy of Mind* (*E*, Pt. 3). Translated by W. Wallace and A. V. Miller. Oxford: Clarendon, 1971.

_____. *Phänomenologie des Geistes.* Edited by J. Hoffmeister. 6th ed. Hamburg: Felix Meiner, 1952. Cited in the text as *PG.* English translation: *Phenomenology of Spirit.* Translated by A. V. Miller. Oxford: Clarendon, 1977. Cited in the text as PS.

_____. *Werke in zwanzig Bänden.* Edited by Eva Moldenhauer and Karl Markus Michel. Frankfurt:Suhrkamp, 1969–70. Cited in the text are the following:

TW2: Jenaer Schriften 1801–1807.

TW7: Grundlinien der Philosophie des Rechts. Cited as *PdR.* English translation: *Hegel's Philosophy of Right*. Translated by T. M. Knox. Oxford: Clarendon, 1952. Cited as PoR.

TW11: Berliner Schriften 1818-1831.

TW16-17: Vorlesungen über die Philosophie der Religion.

_____. *Wissenschaft der Logik*. 2 Vols. Edited by G. Lasson. 3rd ed. Hamburg: Felix Meiner, 1971, 1975. Cited as *L1*, *L2*. English translation: *Hegel's Science of Logic*. Translated by A. V. Miller. New York: Humanities Press, 1969. Cited as SL.

Heidegger, Martin. *Schellings Abhandlung über das Wesen der menschlichen Freiheit*. Edited by H. Feick. Tübingen: Max Niemeyer, 1972.

Heinrichs, Johannes. *Die Logik der 'Phänomenologie des Geistes.'* Bonn: Bouvier, 1974.

Henrich, Dieter. "Formen der Negation in Hegels Logik." *Hegel-Jahrbuch* (1974): 245-256.

_____. *Hegel im Kontext*. Frankfurt: Suhrkamp, 1971.

_____. "Hegels Grundoperation." In *Der Idealismus und seine Gegenwart. Festschrift für Werner Marx zum 65. Geburtstag*, pp. 208-230. Edited by U. Guzzoni, B. Rang, and L. Siep. Hamburg: Felix Meiner, 1976.

Holz, Harald. *Spekulation und Faktizität. Zum Freiheitsbegriff des mittleren und späten Schelling*. Bonn: Bouvier, 1970.

Hyppolite, Jean. *Genesis and Structure of Hegel's Phenomenology of Spirit*. Evanston: Northwestern University Press, 1974.

Kant, Immanuel. *Kritik der reinen Vernunft*. Edited by Raymund Schmidt. Hamburg: Felix Meiner, 1926; reprint edition 1971. Cited in the text with page numbers from the 1978 (A) and 1878 (B) editions. English translation: *Critique of Pure Reason*. Translated by Norman Kemp Smith. New York: St. Martin's Press, 1965.

_____. *Werke in Zehn Bänden*. Edited by Wilhelm Weischedel. Darmstadt: Wissenschaftliche Buchgesellschaft, 1959. Vol. 5: *Schriften zur Metaphysik und Logik*.

Kasper, Walter. *Das Absolute in der Geschichte: Philosophie und Theologie der Geschichte in der Spätphilosophie Schellings*. Mainz: Matthias-Grünewald-Verlag, 1965.

Kojève, Alexandre. *Introduction to the Reading of Hegel*. New York: Basic Books, 1969.

Kroner, Richard. "Anschauen und Denken: Kritische Bemerkungen zu Rickerts heterothetischem Denkprinzip." *Logos* XIII (1924-25): 90-127.

Labarrière, Pierre-Jean. *Structures et mouvement dialectique dans la Phénoménologie de l'esprit de Hegel*. Paris: Aubier-Montaigne, 1968.

Löwith, Karl. *From Hegel to Nietzsche*. New York: Doubleday, 1967.

Prauss, Gerold. *Einführung in die Erkenntnistheorie*. Darmstadt: Wissenschaftliche Buchgesellschaft, 1980.

_____. *Erscheinung bei Kant. Ein Problem der "Kritik der reinen Vernunft"*. Berlin: Walter de Gruyter, 1971.

_____. *Kant und das Problem der Dinge an sich*. Bonn: Bouvier, 1977.

Rickert, Heinrich. *Das Eine, die Einheit und die Eins*. 2nd ed. Tübingen: Mohr, 1924.

Ritter, Joachim. *Metaphysik und Politik*. Frankfurt: Suhrkamp, 1977.

Rosen, Stanley. *G. W. F. Hegel. An Introduction to the Science of Wisdom*. New Haven: Yale University Press, 1974.

_____. *Nihilism*. New Haven: Yale University Press, 1969.

_____. "Self-Consciousness and Self-Knowledge: The Relation between Plato and Hegel." *Hegel-Studien* 9 (1974): 109–29.

Schelling, Friedrich Wilhelm Joseph. *Grundlegung der positiven Philosophie*. Edited by H. Fuhrmans. Torino: Bottega d'Erasmo, 1972. Cited as *GPP*.

_____. *Sämmtliche Werke*. 14 vols. Stuttgart and Augsburg: J. G. Cotta'scher Verlag, 1856-61; reprint edition of selected works, Darmstadt: Wissenschaftliche Buchgesellschaft, 1974–76. The following listing of works by volume and page number will clarify the references:

1:85–148. "Ueber die Möglichkeit einer Form der Philosophie überhaupt" (1794).

3:327–634. *System der transzendentalen Idealismus* (1800). English translation: *System of Transcendental Idealism*. Translated by Peter Heath. Charlottesville: University of Virginia Press, 1980.

4:105–212. *Darstellung meines Systems der Philosophie* (1801).

4:213–332. *Bruno oder über das göttliche und natürliche Princip der Dinge* (1802).

4:333–510. *Fernere Darstellungen aus dem System der Philosophie* (1802).

6:11–70. "Philosophie und Religion" (1804).

6:131–574. *System der gesammten Philosophie und der Natur-philosophie insbesondere* (1804). 6:215–574 from the Schröder edition (see below).

7:331–416. *Philosophische Untersuchungen über das Wesen der menschlichen Freiheit und die damit zusammenhängende Gegenstände* (1809). English translation: *Of Human Freedom.* Translated by James Gutman. Chicago: Open Court, 1936.

9:353–66. "Erste Vorlesung in München" (1827).

10:1–200. *Zur Geschichte der neueren Philosophie* (c. 1827).

10:201–24. "Vorrede zu einer philosophischen Schrift des Herrn Victor Cousin" (1834).

11:1–252. "Historische-kritische Einleitung in die Philosophie der Mythologie."

11:253–572. "Philosophische Einleitung in die Philosophie der Mythologie oder Darstellung der rein-rationellen Philosophie."

11:573–90. "Abhandlung über die Quelle der ewigen Wahrheiten."

12:1–674. *Philosophie der Mythologie.*

13:1–174. "Einleitung in die Philosophie der Offenbarung oder Begründung der positiven Philosophie."

13:177–530. *Der Philosophie der Offenbarung Erster Teil.*

14:1–334. *Der Philosophie der Offenbarung Zweiter Teil.*

14:335–56. "Andere Deduktion der Principien der positiven Philosophie."

14:357–67. "Erste Vorlesung in Berlin" (1841).

_____. *Sämmtliche Werke.* A second reprint edition of selected works. Edited by Manfred Schröter. Munich: C. H. Beck'sche Verlagsbuchhandlung. Cited from this edition, 6:215–574.

Schneider, Peter K. *Die Wissenschaftsbegründende Funktion der Transzendentalphilosophie.* Freiburg and Munich, 1965.

Schulz, Walter. *Die Vollendung des Deutschen Idealismus in der Spätphilosophie Schellings.* 2nd ed. Pfullingen: Neske, 1975.

Seebohm, Thomas. "The Grammar of Hegel's Dialectic." *Hegel–Studien* 11 (1976): 149–80.

_____. "Das Widerspruchsprinzip in der Kantischen Logik und der Hegelschen Dialektik." In *Akten des 4. Internationalen Kant-Kongresses.* Part II.2: 862–74. Berlin: Walter de Gruyter, 1974.

Schelling. *Une philosophie en devenir.* 2 vols. Paris: Vrin, 1970.

Volkmann-Schluck, Karl-Heinz. *Mythos und Logos. Interpretationen zu Schellings Philosophie der Mythologie.* Berlin: Walter de Gruyter, 1969.

Wagner, Hans. *Philosophie und Reflexion.* 2nd ed. Munich and Basel: Reinhard Verlag, 1959.

White, Alan. *The End of Philosophy: A Study of Schelling and Hegel.*

PhD thesis, The Pennsylvania State University, 1980.

_____. *Schelling: An Introduction to the System of Freedom.* New Haven: Yale University Press, 1983.

Wieland, Wolfgang. *Schellings Lehre von der Zeit. Grundlagen und Voraussetzungen der Weltalterphilosophie.* Heidelberg: Carl Winter Universitätsverlag, 1956.

Index